TEEN BOYS SURVIVAL GUIDE

A Teen Boys Guide for Cultivating Positive Attitude, Develop Critical Thinking Skills, Problem-Solving Abilities, Practice Empathy and Understanding towards Others

V GODFREY

TEEN
Boys
SURVIVAL
GUIDE
A Teen Boys Guide for Cultivating
Positive Attitude, Develop Critical Thinking
Skills, Problem-Solving Abilities,
Practice Empathy and
Understanding towards Others
V GODFREY

TABLE OF CONTENTS

INTRODUCTION

Having the capacity to tackle the constant demands in the present-day continuously changing environment requires developing survival life skills.

The ever-evolving and demanding tech world, plus the tremendous shifts in world economies over the last decade, has had an influence on family life, job, and education.

Because of this, teen boys require new life skills, such as the capacity to develop the right positive attitude, develop strong work ethics, practice empathy and gratitude, set realistic and achievable goals, manage stress and anxiety, and deal with the constantly increasing speed and change of contemporary life.

For their life and career, today's teen boys will have several different occupations with the corresponding demands and need for flexibility.

So, developing and practicing life skills is essential for their mental health, success, and independence.

Teen boys want to transition into strong and independent adults, but they can only thrive and succeed as independent adults if they develop the right life skills.

Becoming an adult might sound interesting, but it comes with its unique problems and challenges. Teen boys may use life skills to help them manage the difficulties and demands of everyday life, from controlling their emotions to making wise decisions.

They may also grow in terms of personality, capabilities, and physical and mental prowess and fulfill their full potential.

The essential learning instrument for survival, capacity growth, and a great life is life skills. Gaining life skills promotes healthy social, emotional, and cognitive development.

The promotion of mental health in teen boys aids in the growth of emotional intelligence, self-confidence and the improvement of decision-making, critical thinking, and creative thinking skills.

The life skills they possess will aid in fostering a cheerful and adaptable outlook on things since life skills provide us the ability to adapt to different circumstances while boosting our self-esteem and confidence.

Life skills are something we pick up via experience. And everyone is born with the capacity for life skills, but to maximize potential, we need to sharpen them routinely.

By improving our life skills, we can respond to circumstances and other life challenges, enabling us to live a wholesome and happy life.

Understanding the value of life skills is necessary if we wish to lead successful lives.

Additionally, it is crucial to put it into practice in our daily lives, and if this occurs, our life may proceed straightforwardly and beneficially. We become capable of making our lives simple and easy, creating a good existence, and making the most of our time through developing life skills.

Life skills are crucial in our daily lives because they sharpen the capacity for situational adaptation and societal success in all spheres. Life skills are essential in life. Thus, it's vital to address their lack in the lives of teen boys. Lack of life skills affects relationships, academic success, and future careers.

The good thing is that this book contains the life skills teen boys need to navigate life's daily challenges and transition to successful and independent adults.

CHAPTER 1

DEVELOPING GOOD COMMUNICATION SKILLS

Humans have a responsibility to each other and engage in some forms of communication. Each person plays a variety of roles every day, depending on the circumstances of a given engagement.

Every contact requires good communication, which all interactions must have. Recognizing body language clues and having good listening skills are two components that go into building and sustaining authentic, long-lasting relationships via communication.

One may see an enhancement in the standard of social interactions as well as an increase in confidence while interacting with people in a social capacity by adequately using these skills. These advantages may be crucial for landing a job or creating enduring and healthy relationships.

One of the most essential social skills for everybody to have to thrive in the world is communication skills.

When you communicate effectively, you ensure the other person receives your message and emotions. Effective communication makes it easier for people to complete life responsibilities with family, friends, or coworkers.

When communication is successful, everyone engaged feels content and accomplished, and delivering communications eliminates the possibility of misinterpretation or message modification, reducing the likelihood of conflict.

Effective communication is essential for ensuring that conflicts are addressed in a courteous way when they do occur. To get a job, keep a good relationship, and healthily express oneself, one's communication skills may make or break such endeavors.

How to Develop Effective Communication Skills

Successful communication is essential for success in many facets of life. Good communication skills are vital for success in relationships, education, and many occupations.

Good communicators have more positive relationships with their friends and family. As a result, effective interpersonal communication is essential, and understanding how to do so has several advantages. However, a lot of people need help with where to begin.

Here are some tips for enhancing your communication skills.

1. Focused Listening

Listening is one of the most vital skills that need development since everyone has a propensity to overlook the fact that communication is an exchange of information.

We get into the "broadcasting" trap when we send a message without paying attention to the reaction. We often find ourselves thinking about what we want to say next in a discussion rather than listening to the other person.

Your relationships at school, work, and home will likely improve as your listening skills improve.

What are listening skills?

Hearing and listening are not the same thing. Learning to listen is paying attention to not just the words being spoken but also the way they are being said and any accompanying nonverbal cues. It entails giving the person speaking your undivided attention and paying close attention to both what they are saying in addition to what they are not saying.

To corroborate what the other individual has said and clear up any misunderstandings, good listeners utilize the strategies of explanation and reflection. Like active listening, these approaches also make it highly evident that you are listening.

2. Learning about and comprehending nonverbal communication.

Nonverbal cues play a big part in any message's transmission. According to some research, it might account for as much as Eighty percent of the conversation.

Therefore, it is crucial to take into account and comprehend non-verbal communication—especially when it is lacking or diminished, as when communicating in writing or over the phone. Although body language is frequently considered nonverbal communication, it encompasses much more.

It encompasses things like speech inflection and intonation, body language, eye contact, posture, and even changes in the body like perspiration.

By carefully observing how others communicate nonverbally, you can better comprehend them. Consistency in your language and body language will also help your message get through more effectively.

3. Emotional Intelligence and Control.

The third underappreciated aspect of communication is the capacity to manage our emotions and those of others. It is easy to fall into the trap of believing everything should be rational and that emotion has no place at work or school.

But because we are human, we are emotional. None of us can and shouldn't attempt to leave our emotions at home. Not that we should "let it all hang out," either.

However, conscious awareness of good and bad emotions can undoubtedly enhance communication.

Emotional intelligence is the ability to recognize our emotions and those of others. There is a lot of evidence to suggest that it is far more crucial to succeeding in life than what we may term "intellectual intelligence."

Typically divided into social and personal skills, emotional intelligence encompasses a wide range of abilities.

The personal skills are motivation, self-awareness, and self-regulation. And social skills have to do with empathy.

For instance: Emotional awareness, correct self-evaluation, and self-assurance are all components of self-awareness.

Empathy is the capacity to "feel with" others, to experience and comprehend their feelings. It entails developing others, appreciating the variety and using it to one's advantage, and being self-conscious when communicating with others.

Fundamentally, the idea underlying the many skills that contribute to emotional intelligence is that you must be aware of, understand, and control your emotions to comprehend and get along with others.

4. Questioning skills

Questioning is a problematic area that many individuals encounter, and to make sure you have gotten someone's message accurately, questioning is an important skill. It is also a highly effective approach to learning more about a specific subject or to begin and maintain a discussion.

As a result of their propensity to spend far more time gathering information from others than airing their viewpoints, people with solid questioning skills are sometimes seen as having excellent listening skills.

5. Be concise and straightforward.

The choice of words is the central aspect of communication. Less is more when it pertains to word choice as well. Clarity and, where feasible, conciseness are the keys to effective and convincing communication, whether it be in writing or speaking.

Prior to communicating in any way, identify your audience and objectives. To make sure you include all relevant information, carefully and thoroughly lay out what you want to say and why. It will also assist you in removing extraneous data.

Keep your wording simple; flowery or needless phrases might detract from your point, and although repetition could be required in certain circumstances, be sure to use it sparingly. Your audience will be more likely to hear your message if you repeat it; however, too much repetition risks losing their attention.

6. Prepare in advance.

Before starting any conversation, prepare what and how you will say it. But being ready goes beyond simply practicing a presentation.

Additionally, planning entails considering the entire communication from beginning to end. Do some research on the data you may need to back up your points and think about your response to inquiries and remarks.

Make an effort to foresee the unexpected. Create a list of possible questions, requests for more details or explanations, and arguments before starting any discussion so you are prepared to deal with them rationally and concisely.

7. Observe your tone.

Even more significant than what you say is how you say it. Like other nonverbal signals, your tone may either strengthen and emphasize your message or ultimately detract from it.

The tone may be particularly significant when there is a dispute or disagreement at school, home, or work. A well-chosen term with a pleasant meaning and tone fosters trust and goodwill. A poorly selected term with an ambiguous or unfavorable tone may cause misunderstandings very fast.

The tone in speech refers to the loudness, intonation, and word choice used while speaking.

It might be challenging to manage tone in real-time so that it reflects your goal. However, being aware of your tone will help you adjust it when necessary if communication looks like it is going in the opposite direction.

Writing can make tone control simpler. Make sure to read your communication aloud once, if not twice, keeping tone and message in mind. If doing so won't compromise confidentially, you could even wish to read it aloud or have a trusted friend do so.

Additionally, avoid responding in a hurried manner when exchanging words via e-mail or another written medium. Write your answer if feasible, but wait to e-mail it for a day or two. Rereading your letter after your emotions have subsided often enables you to control your tone to lessen the likelihood of the argument escalating.

8. Don't be afraid to express your opinions.

Make sure you're expressing your own needs, just as it's critical to comprehend what others are looking for. No one will ever find out if you don't tell them, right?

This communication ability is crucial if you're a team leader since what you say will determine how your team will behave. You provide an example for others to follow by being honest and forthright communicators.

They will be more inclined to cooperate with you, make concessions when they are called for, and approach challenging circumstances with an optimistic outlook on how things will turn out in the end.

9. Try to avoid assuming anything.

It's simple to think you know another person's desires. But this is a significant contributor to misunderstandings, so that miscommunications can become conflicts.

Active listening skills may come to the rescue in this situation. Empathy, or attempting to comprehend other people's thinking, is a crucial component of excellent communication skills. It is significant since what we say needs to reflect what we truly desire accurately.

We often attempt to cover up or conceal our actual wants, especially when things are tough or it's simple to get frustrated or humiliated. You may significantly reduce misconceptions and the likelihood of confrontation by asking questions, paying attention to the responses, and repeating what you believe they want.

10. Develop self-awareness, particularly during complicated interactions.

Advanced communicators have a strong understanding of their own emotions. They know how to manage them when they get agitated or too eager and prevent them from dominating the discussion or creating an unneeded commotion.

When responding to something you don't like, it's critical to maintain composure. Stop if you feel your face flushed or your heart racing.

Attempt to locate some quiet time where you may relax. Knowing when to accept that you are mistaken is another essential component of self-awareness.

Although it might feel like an enormous hit to your ego, I promise you'll find that by owning up to your mistakes and doing your best to avoid repeating them in the future, you'll gain the respect and integrity of your family, friends, and coworkers.

11. When bringing up a concern, avoid becoming accusatory.

A problematic circumstance will inevitably arise. Maintain your composure while you have the conversation, even if you believe the other person did anything that was blatantly improper. If you begin the discussion by blaming them for anything, it's a call for a quarrel.

We tend to get defensive in response to accusations, and that debate seldom ends well.

For instance, when something has only happened a few times, refrain from stating they "always" or "never" do it. Instead, please stick to the facts, show empathy, and shift the conversation to how to remedy it.

Try saying something like, "I notice on the attendance list that you have been late twice this week," Is everything all right?" Rather than, "You're usually late for meetings."

It gives you the opportunity to determine what could be amiss and how you might contribute to preventing it from occurring again.

Enhancing Non-verbal Communication Skills

12. Maintain eye contact

When someone is speaking, look them in the eye. The best advice for demonstrating that you are listening to someone is to do this. Maintain constant eye contact without seeming weird.

It is a delicate balance. Stay away from distracting gestures and fidgeting. Avoid seven readjustments in your chair, and avoid repeatedly clicking your pen open and shut.

Avoid flipping through your documents or opening new tabs on your computer while communicating with another person.

13. Keep a straight spine.

Another of those advice pieces appears essential yet is shockingly simple to ignore.

When communicating with others, maintain a good posture by keeping your spine straight. Don't communicate with your arms crossed. It is considered by some to be a "power stance."

It may be the case in certain circumstances, but in others, it may give the impression that you are far from the other individual. It might come across as impatient to leave, which isn't conducive to fruitful conversation.

Enhancing Written Communication Skills

Never reply to texts when feeling angry.

Have you ever been angry when you wrote an e-mail, then afterward thought, "Damn it, how come I said that?

Take a five- to ten-minute timeout after receiving an upsetting message to collect yourself before responding. Your relationships may benefit significantly from this.

Create e-mail subject lines and titles that are descriptive. Think of how irritating it is to receive an e-mail with "(no subject)"?"

Use as few words and as much specificity as you can in your e-mail titles to inform them of their precise contents.

14. Keep your phrases and words simple.

As a general guideline, your sentences should be at most two lines long.

Please take advantage of every chance to halve or shorten them. Additionally, it would be best if you refrained from overusing big words that individuals might find confusing in your writing.

Be succinct and to the point. A lengthy, winding e-mail isn't as delightful as sharing a long, winding narrative face to face, just because neither situation is ideal.

It increases the likelihood that people will skim over or outright ignore critical facts, which not only makes them feel like you're wasting their time but also increases the likelihood that they will overlook them.

How Take Care of your Hygiene and Grooming is next in Chapter 2. Happy Reading.

CHAPTER 2

TAKE CARE OF YOUR HYGIENE AND GROOMING

You may have a lot of knowledge about the world for a teenage boy, but there is always more to discover. For instance, you presumably understand personal hygiene and why it is crucial, but how thoroughly have you investigated the subject?

Your goal should be to perfect personal hygiene. Every kid should be aware of this vital skill. Read on to understand what you need about personal hygiene and grooming.

What Is Personal Hygiene?

The word "personal hygiene" refers to all of the things you do to look after your body. Typically, it emphasizes hygiene and overall health. Therefore, activities like taking a shower, brushing your teeth, shaving, and applying deodorant all contribute to your hygiene.

Please list all the activities in your daily schedule that you consider to be hygienic. You'll discover there is more than you would anticipate.

Importance of Personal Hygiene

Personal hygiene is essential, to put it simply. It has an effect on your physical well-being, social interactions, and self-esteem. Even in times of stress, maintaining proper hygiene may keep you healthy and content.

To begin with, maintaining cleanliness aids in illness prevention. According to research, the typical individual touches their face twenty-three times each hour. Those touches are much less likely to make you ill if you practice good hygiene.

Additionally, hygiene affects how your body and clothing smell. Although you are aware that you have no desire to be the smelly kid, you may not realize how simple it is to smell bad, particularly during times of hormonal change.

You won't have an issue with folks avoiding you outright because you make their eyes wet since your cleanliness will keep you feeling fresh.

Personal hygiene also makes you feel clean. These provide your brain with feel-good chemicals known for positive reinforcement.

It's time to develop a plan now that you are aware of the benefits that good personal hygiene may provide for you.

You are swiftly approaching adulthood, and there will be a few minor modifications, but your hygiene routine will be comparable to an adult's.

I will review valuable and important hygiene advice for teen boys, including essential grooming and personal hygiene practices.

Personal Hygiene Tips for Teen Boys

Maintaining good hygiene is essential for teen boys to social interaction and self-care.

Here are some crucial personal hygiene tips to follow.

1. Frequently wash your hands.

One of the best methods to stop the transmission of germs is to wash your hands.

Before eating, immediately after using the restroom, and participating in activities that might have subjected your hands to germs, wash your hands with water and soap to prevent infection.

2. Regularly take a bath.

Bathing may assist in reducing body odor by removing sweat, grime, and germs from the skin. Aim to take a shower a minimum of twice a day, more often if you're exercising or sweating easily.

3. Utilize deodorant.

By killing the microorganisms that produce odor, deodorant aids in the prevention of body odor. After showering, select a deodorant that suits you and administer it to your underarms. Remember that deodorants only function when you thoroughly cleanse your armpits; using them on grimy armpits is not suggested.

4. Brush your teeth twice daily

Plaque removal and gum and tooth decay prevention are aided by brushing your teeth two times a day. Use fluoride-containing toothpaste, and be sure you brush for a minimum of two minutes each time.

5. Consistently wash your clothing

Make washing your clothing often a habit, and you shouldn't dress in soiled attire.

You should wash your clothes as soon as they become noticeably dirty or odorous, and if possible, wash your clothes after each use, especially if you sweat a lot.

It would be best if you washed your underwear after each use. So that you consistently have something clean to wear, keep a pile of clean clothing.

6. Regularly trim your nails.

Regular nail trimming helps to avoid the accumulation of dirt and germs beneath the nails. Clip your nails evenly using a nail clipper or pair of scissors, and ensure to clean underneath them with a toothbrush or nail brush.

7. Moisturize your skin.

Your skin may avoid dryness, flakiness, and discomfort by being moisturized. After taking a shower, select a moisturizer suitable for your skin type and administer it to your face and body.

8. Maintain your hair.

As a teenager, taking good care of your hair is exceptionally crucial. Your hair must be clean, regardless of whether you want to let it grow out or keep it short.

It involves brushing your hair daily and using a quality hair product to hydrate and smooth it.

9. Sleep well and enough

When you don't get enough sleep, your body's defense systems that keep you healthy all breakdown. Despite the fact that most teenagers often lack sleep, you don't have to be one of those people.

A few actions can help you sleep better.

- Reduce your caffeine intake, particularly after supper.
- Speaking about supper, it helps to eat sooner in the evening and refrain from consuming late-night snacks. When you are overweight, your sleep will be less restful.
- Dim or turn off the light before going to bed.
- Avoid using electronics an hour before bed.

Establish a Skin Care Regimen

A skin care regimen benefits you in many ways. It first aids in overall cleanliness maintenance. It lessens your tendency to get ill or develop infections, particularly on your skin.

You'll feel more comfortable all around because of your regimen, which also prevents your skin from becoming dry and harsh. Since you aren't constantly battling discomfort and itchiness, this will assist with your general psychological well-being.

We can condense a proper regimen into four stages (in addition to the apparent need for bathing) for the reasons listed above.

Step 1
Utilize a cleanser to clean your face.

In a pinch, you can wash your face with different soaps, but using something explicitly made for a human face is preferable. The purpose is that using plenty of soaps can dry out your skin, which on your face will worsen issues like acne and dandruff in your facial hair.

Furthermore, the chemical composition of a soap that is great for every part of your body and is chemically healthy for your face will differ. So the first step is to purchase and use a suitable facial cleanser.

Step 2
Moisturize your face

Showering and other personal hygiene practices may lead to dry skin, regardless of whether you use a decent face wash

It would be best if you moisturize your face. Because a facial moisturizer will be less fragrant, and it helps to hydrate your face.

Step 3
Exfoliate

Exfoliating your skin is the third stage, but let's go more specific.

Only about once a week should you exfoliate. Overdoing it may be detrimental.

By exfoliating, you remove debris, dead skin cells, and other substances that may block the pores. Maintaining clear pores enables your skin to heal itself.

Step 4
Avoid harm behaviors

The last stage requires a bit more work. Avoiding harmful behaviors is essential. It's wise to consider your nutrition as it might cause skin issues and breakouts.

Touching your face—something we all do more often than we used to—can boost oil production and contribute to the development of acne.

Long-term stressful activities might result in acne and less-than-healthy skin. So look at your regimen and see whether there are any behaviors you can change to keep your face clear and clean.

Learning how to handle Conflict in a Productive and Peaceful Manner is next in Chapter 3. See you there.

CHAPTER 3

LEARN TO HANDLE CONFLICT IN A PRODUCTIVE AND PEACEFUL MANNER

Conflicts may occur when there is a direct difference of opinion or interest. Thus, it's critical to know how to handle and settle them. There are various situations when conflict may arise between friends and colleagues at school, at home, and work, and when it takes place, it's critical to deal with it quickly before it worsens.

I go through peaceful dispute resolution techniques, how to use them, and the advantages of conflict resolution in this chapter.

Conflict resolution skills are necessary while acting professionally since conflict is often a result of human connection. When a conflict emerges, the most beneficial course of action is to employ peaceful negotiation to settle the issue.

What is conflict resolution?

Conflict may sometimes arise from human connection, hence resolving it requires conflict resolution skills.

Both sides can resolve their conflict via negotiation or conflict resolution, leaving everyone feeling somewhat pleased. Sometimes the person who settles a dispute is a third party or mediator, while other times, it may be a participant who uses an objective eye to find a resolution.

A common perception of leadership is the capacity to settle disputes. Many businesses value the skills of individuals who can spot conflict, respect divergent viewpoints, and forge agreement.

The Importance of Conflict Resolution

Effective conflict resolution has a variety of advantages, including:

1. Fosters enduring and healthy relationships

Effective conflict resolution techniques may help to lessen any unhappiness that can harm friendships, and relationships, promote improved teamwork among colleagues, and ultimately build solid working connections among employees.

2. Upholds harmony and morale

Effective conflict resolution may stop animosity between opposing workers from escalating and affecting other employees who weren't initially engaged.

A speedy, courteous conclusion may assist in preserving harmony among friends and morale at work and help avoid interruptions in production.

3. Realizes Goals

Conflict resolution may improve productivity and assist parties in achieving their goals. Following a solution, they enhance their friendship or are able to work more productively—and together—by concentrating on the desired outcomes instead of the conflict.

4. Lessens stress

Resolving a conflict may help those involved, as well as their parents, instructors, and other coworkers and customers, feel less stressed

Stress management is crucial for both physical and mental health. Additionally, people who are less stressed find it simpler to concentrate and participate in their roles.

5. Offers understanding

Conflict resolution offers the chance to comprehend a distinct viewpoint. It's sometimes possible to get fresh ideas by discussing the causes of someone else's perspective that differ from yours. These ideas help you become a more tolerant person or assist you in finding fresh approaches to difficulties.

6. Strengthens teamwork in the workplace

If there is conflict at work, staff members may be more inclined to look for alternative employment. By encouraging them to remain, conflict resolution may help the business maintain the expertise and experience of its seasoned staff.

Guidelines for using conflict resolution techniques

Here are some pointers for successful conflict resolution skills.

- Establish ground rules, such as requiring both parties to avoid using "you" terms that might suggest responsibility.
- Engage in active listening and convey via body language that you are paying attention and nodding.
- To gain and keep the respect of all parties, always behave honestly and objectively.
- Only meet with individuals in groups. Group meetings make sure there are no lingering questions about any preferential treatment that may have taken place behind closed doors.
- Recognize when to take some time off, when your emotions are high, or when your nerves need to settle down.
- If necessary, bring in a third party to serve as a mediator since doing so will demonstrate your honesty and win you respect from all parties.

Effective Techniques for Mediating Conflict

1. Speak honestly

If there is no imminent danger of physical harm, speak with the individual you are having an issue with face-to-face. Instead of writing a letter, pounding on the wall, flinging a rock, or whining to everyone else, having a direct dialogue is considerably more successful.

2. Pick a suitable moment.

Make a schedule and provide enough time to have a talk. Don't, for instance, bring up the argument as the other individual is ready to leave to do something vital. Try to have the conversation in a peaceful setting where you both feel at ease and unbothered for whatever long it lasts.

3. Make plans.

Prepare your speech by thinking about it beforehand. Please describe the issue and how it impacts you.

4. Avoid blaming or disparaging others.

It is impossible for the other person to hear you and comprehend your worries if you start an argument with them. Don't start the discussion by blaming the other individual for everything or suggesting a course of action.

5. Provide details

Don't make assumptions about how others are acting. Such as, "You are purposefully obstructing my vision to irritate me!"

Give details about your emotions instead: I am angry when you obstruct my vision because I can't see what the instructor is writing.

6. Show understanding

Allow the other party to explain their argument fully. Sit back, listen, and try to understand the other individual's feelings.

Demonstrate your listening skills. Even if you disagree with what the other person is saying, let them know you heard them and appreciate that you are talking about the issue.

7. Discuss it thoroughly.

Once you get going, express all of your problems and emotions. Don't ignore the information that looks "complicated" to communicate or "insignificant" to be significant. The more completely you address all the problems, the better your solutions will be.

8. Develop a resolution.

Once the conversation reaches this point, you should begin formulating a solution. One person instructing another to change is far less successful than two or more individuals working together.

9. Take action

Please set up a schedule for checking in with each other to make sure that the agreement stays in effect, and then stick to it.

10. Remain composed and display stable body language.

Taking a couple of deep breaths before you start might be beneficial. You may also relax by drawing your shoulders back and sitting down rather than standing, and instead of crossing your feet, you might put them both on the ground. Instead of crossing your arms or moving them, keep them open and at your sides.

11. Accept there is an issue.

It is beneficial for everyone first to acknowledge that there is an issue to have the greatest opportunity of having a fruitful talk.

Start the conflict-resolution process by gently outlining your perspective and inviting the opposing party or parties to elaborate. Use "I" sentences rather than "You don't pay attention to my suggestions" when expressing how you feel.

Create a space where everyone may freely express their opinions rather than placing the blame for the disagreement on a specific person.

12. Agree to agree.

After the issue has been understood, everyone must concur that a solution is necessary.

Suppose you are resolving a dispute, and one party is reluctant to join the settlement process. In that case, speak with them privately to better understand their position and how you might persuade them to participate.

13. Attempt to comprehend everyone's point of view.

The majority of confrontations at home, school, and work do not involve malicious intent. Instead, misunderstandings are the primary cause of most conflicts.

It might be simpler to settle a dispute if you take the time to pay attention to and comprehend other people's experiences.

14. Note the circumstances that led to the argument.

Conflict may have resulted from several unidentified stresses on people. Deadlines, fatigue, family, health, hunger, burnout, and other factors may all cause heightened emotions that spark conflict. It might be helpful to negotiate or prevent a possible dispute in the future if you are aware of the triggers and stresses of the other persons involved.

15. Look for chances to compromise.

Most disputes need at least one party to accept a compromise to be resolved.

At this point in the resolution, the ability to put aside ego or stubbornness is crucial, and if all sides can find a way to compromise in some manner, the outcome will feel the greatest to everyone concerned. So, look for places where compromise is conceivable as you get closer to a conclusion.

16. Come upon a resolution strategy.

At this stage, everyone should be thinking about how they played a role in the problem and the things they can do to fix it. Before you stop talking, try to come up with a plan for resolving the issue that includes actions for each party.

Apologies and behavior modifications may be part of the settlement strategy to avoid the same issue from happening again. For instance, if a worker believes their boss doesn't appreciate their ideas, a resolution strategy can include the manager scheduling a one-on-one meeting to listen to suggestions that the worker has recorded during the week.

17. Verify if the agreement is enduring by checking in.

Conflict resolution requires follow-through. Even if the talk went well, its significance would only be recovered if the plan for settlement was carried through.

Establishing a check-in point to review how everybody feels and ensure that everybody is adhering to the agreed-upon plan within a couple of weeks or days can help set expectations.

In Chapter 4, you will learn how to Develop Good Teamwork skills, and the Fun Activities that will Help you Develop Good Teamwork skills. See you there.

CHAPTER 4

DEVELOP GOOD TEAMWORK SKILLS

While some teens can get along with their fellow students or a group, others may find it difficult to cooperate as a team.

Teen team-building exercises are a fantastic method to educate teens on the value of cooperation and to develop their leadership abilities. Several entertaining games and activities might come to your aid and assist you in acquiring the social skills necessary for teamwork.

In this chapter, I'll share several team-building exercises that may help teen boys develop self-awareness, trust, and the ability to work as a team.

The Importance of Teamwork Skills

1. Build connections

Teenagers learn how to engage with others as they participate in a team-building exercise. These activities introduce them to the idea of unique views, which is a crucial component of social skills.

2. Improve communication skills

Some adolescent introverts find communication difficult and may find it beneficial to learn how to interact with others via team-building exercises and games.

3. Motivate

Teenagers may benefit significantly from their friends' encouragement, according to research.

Kids have the chance to get motivated to work on a specific assignment by participating in team-building games or activities with their peers or classmates.

4. Encourage productivity

Working as a team requires generating and combining several ideas to solve the current issue. Adolescents may utilize this working method to increase productivity and efficiency by identifying their strengths and shortcomings.

5. Build critical thinking skills.

Teenagers discover several approaches to handling an issue when they participate in the exercise. It broadens their reasoning and problem-solving ability, essential for accomplishing a task.

6. Increases Cooperation

Through team-building exercises, you will learn to work together with various groups of individuals to accomplish a shared objective.

7. Allows for feedback

Teenagers have the chance to hear criticism and make positive use of it.

8. Enhances leadership potential

These activities foster a feeling of independence and accountability and aid in the development of the teen's leadership abilities.

Teen Boys Teamwork Building Games and Activities

These team-building exercises and games focus on many aspects of growth, including problem-solving, decision-making, flexibility, planning, and trust-building.

These fun teamwork-building activities can be done with adults, teachers, and young adults

1. "Boo the dragon"

Create teams of six to seven adolescents apiece. One adolescent performs the dragon and therefore assumes the role of the judge.

In the game, teenagers must frighten away a dragon attacking their village, where they dwell. Every squad corresponds to a community. While wearing blindfolds, the villagers must arrange themselves from tallest to smallest.

They may talk among themselves and experiment with different techniques to quickly form a line of people in ascending order of height.

The team must cooperatively yell "Boo!" to frighten the monster off. The team that completes the assignment first yells "Boo!" "to the dragon. Wins the game

2. Line up in silence.

Depending on specific qualities, the participants must line up. You may, for instance, ask each youngster to stand according to the size of their shoes.

As a result, the person with the smallest shoe size will be first in line, and the person with the largest shoe size will be last. The twist in this situation is that they are required to position themselves in a specific manner without speaking to one another.

3. Electric fence

This game focuses on trust and effective collaboration, where each player must exercise critical thinking.

Form groups of four or five people each. Tie a rope off the ground at a certain height. It is an image of the electric fence.

Now give each team a certain amount of time, say 30 seconds, to safely jump the rope and pass the "electric fence" without walking on the rope. You may let each team work independently before comparing the results to determine which team completed the assignment first.

4. Team together to crate

Select a finished product or project that consists of a number of components. For instance, you might ask the group to create a storybook for young children in which each adolescent would be required to write a portion of the narrative. Their ability to collaborate will improve as they work together on a project or objective. Additionally, the teens will discover the value of effective communication.

5. Unknot

Instruct the teenagers to shut their eyes, stand in a circle, and extend their arms. Once they have done that, instruct them to hold hands with anyone nearby without considering whose hand they are holding. The difficulty would then be to untangle the human knot without letting go of the hand they were holding since the hands would have become entangled.

Teenagers will have to cooperate in weaving over and under one another. Through effective communication, this game promotes the ability to make decisions more quickly and accurately. It is one of the most fantastic illustrations of a game or activity that improves communication between people.

6. Paintballing

Physical stamina is required for this demanding team exercise. For some teenagers, paintballing could seem a little too violent. However, it may also be enjoyable.

You need two teams to play the game. Each team will get a certain amount of colored balloons. Each team's job is to attempt to paint each other squad member by throwing these balloons at them.

The participant who is covered in color after being struck by the colored balloon will be removed. In this manner, one side must remove the most members from the other team.

By deliberately organizing as a team, each team member has the ability to cooperate, defend themselves, and protect one another.

7. Photo finish

Ask each participant to stand on one side of a straight line you have drawn on the ground. When you say "go," they must all cross the border simultaneously.

Although it seems simple, it is not. To figure out how they can all cross the line at precisely the same moment needs some trial and error and imaginative problem-solving. If you record the game in pictures or movies, it will be more enjoyable.

8. "The egg drop"

Give the players a carton of fresh eggs and an abundance of home supplies. They must construct the container in which they will drop the egg with the home items offered.

Here, keeping the egg from breaking is the main objective. Asking the participant to stand on something tall, like a chair, before dumping the egg will make the task more difficult. It is an excellent opportunity to show your teen the benefits of thinking creatively.

9. "The future antique"

Divide the participants into a few teams to start the game. A pile of broken mugs, pipe cleaners, cardboard boxes, a broken watch, and other miscellaneous home items should be chosen by each team, and they should then invent a tale about the object being discovered as an "antique" 1000 years from now.

It should take five minutes to finish the whole procedure. The difficulty of this activity encourages your adolescent to collaborate. Teens must communicate clearly and quickly to do this, and a leader must successfully organize this communication.

10. "Draw back-t0-back"

Start this fun exercise by randomly pairing up the teenagers, with each couple representing a team. With their backs turned away, each team member sits back-to-back with their partner.

One adolescent will get a blank sheet of paper, pen, or marker. The other teen will get a piece of paper with a drawing or shape.

Without looking at the other teen, the teen who receives the illustration must verbally describe the drawing to the latter.

The other person is expected to follow verbal directions and sketch the artwork alone. The winning team is the one that completes the assignment first.

11. 'The baggy skit."

It is an enjoyable activity that often makes people laugh a lot. Additionally, it gives teenagers a fantastic chance to recognize each team member's advantages and disadvantages and make use of them for the sake of the group.

Divide the teenagers into teams of four or five people to begin the game. Give each team a bag containing three to four everyday goods. Now, each team must use the things as props in a skit.

The winning team is the one that makes the best use of the resources. It will be a good idea to record each team's skit so that the teenagers may watch it later and savor the experience.

12. Creeping closer

This exercise may help the kid become more perceptive and foster good competitive traits. Create teams out of the adolescents, with one youngster representing each team as "captain." The captain must stand facing the wall or fence on one side of the play area.

The remaining contestants balance themselves on one leg at the other end of the fence or wall. Getting to the captain is the goal of the game. The players silently begin to quietly hop toward the captain when the captain calls, "Start."

The players must freeze if the captain turns around. When the captain turns around, the crew keeps hopping to get to the leader. The whole team must start again in their starting position if the captain observes anybody leaving their job or falling.

13. Human pyramids

It is a strenuous outdoor exercise that demands both cooperation and stamina. This activity can strengthen the bonds between team members through collaboration, excellent leadership, and effective communication.

Divide the teenagers into teams of four or five people to begin the game. Then, within a certain amount of time, say five minutes, each team builds a human pyramid.

Three team members go on all fours to form the first layer, while the next three get onto their backs to form the second layer. Team members should assemble in a circle within the pyramid and face inward.

14. A treasure hunt

Teens will like this entertaining exercise since it makes them laugh and chuckle a lot.

Divide the teenagers into teams of four to five for the game. Request that each team form a straight line and face the same way.

To form a line, each youngster puts their hands on the shoulder of the teen in front of them. The teenager in front of the queue has blindfolds on.

Disperse various things around the space or field. While keeping the line open, each team must collect these items.

The team members not wearing blindfolds provide orders to the front ender, such as "Move right," "Take three steps ahead," and so on. The winning team is the one that completes the mission in the shortest time.

15. Jigsaw puzzle

Divide a jigsaw puzzle into manageable pieces. Give these jigsaw pieces to the various teams within a team. The goal of each sub-team is to finish the problem as soon as feasible. Once finished, each sub-team collaborates with the others to finish the large puzzle that is the entire picture.

Teens' ability to solve problems is improved by participating in this exercise. Additionally, it aids in the growth of collaboration and cooperation, both essential for achieving more outstanding teamwork ethics.

16. Blanket volleyball

This game is the epitome of cooperation and collaboration. You must split the teenagers into two teams for this game. Give each team a sizable blanket or sheet.

Each side must toss the ball over the net to the other team, which must then catch it with a blanket or sheet. The winning team is the one with the most catches.

17. Blind Pictionary

This straightforward yet entertaining team-building project teaches teens how to work together by identifying and maximizing the team's strengths.

Divide the teenagers into two teams to begin the task. Each team will now create a picture on the board in turn. The twist in this scenario is that the drawing teammate will be wearing a blindfold.

Therefore, as he sketches the image, the judge whispers to them their teammates must recognize it. The winning team will be the one that correctly predicts the most images. You may also specify a time restriction to make the game more challenging.

18. Construct a bridge

Each team must carefully use the available resources to fulfill the main task within the allotted time.

Make two teams out of the teenagers in the group. Give each team a bucket of water and a construction kit filled with materials like, putty, pop sticks, twine, paper clips, etc.

Ask the group to construct a bridge that crosses the water bowl in 20 minutes. Each team will put stones on its bridge at the conclusion of the time limit to show how sturdy it is. The team that wins receives a reward, while the bridge that collapses first loses the game.

19. Find the difference

Form two teams out of the players. Request that the first team form a line and face the second team. The second team has a specific time, say five minutes, to assess the opposing team's appearance.

The first team will make ten changes to the second team once their allotted time has passed and they have left the room. The ten items must be discernible.

The second team is required to study the first team once again and list the ten items that have changed when they arrive. The team with the most points wins. Each accurate guess or identification earns one point.

20. "Looped to rope."

Make two groups out of teenagers. There should be a minimum of five people in each group. For the game, make a large rope circle for each team and place it on the ground.

Each team must hold their hands in the air while standing at the circle's perimeter with the rope tight around its ankles. Each team member must move to work the rope up from their ankles to their wrists while always keeping their hands in the air.

The team member will have to maneuver about to slide the rope up. Team members must help to keep the rope as tight as possible.

The winning team is the one that completes the task first, and this enjoyable exercise improves your ability to communicate and solve problems.

21. Lap sit

A group of more than ten players would be ideal for this game.

Ask the teenagers to form a circle and face in the other direction. Tell the participants to advance toward the circle with their left leg turned inside, enlarging the circle as they do so. The players continue to approach one another until their sides are in contact.

The players place their hands on the shoulders of the person in front of them after the count of three. Then instruct them to take a leisurely seat. If the teams follow the instructions exactly, they will finish up on each other's laps. It is a beneficial team-building activity that improves communication and social skills.

22. Chicken, rice, and dogs

Create teams out of the players. Each team will have one person play the part of a farmer, with the other team members playing the part of villagers.

The farmer must take a boat across a river to go home with their purchases, which include a dog, rice, and chicken. The farmer's limited space aboard the boat presents a problem, however.

The farmer must prevent the chicken from eating the rice and the dog from eating the chicken.

So, how does he safely acquire all three purchases? The villages may assist him in coming up with a solution.

The group that finishes the assignment first wins. The ideal brainteaser for encouraging kids to think imaginatively is this game.

23. Tug-of-war

Form two teams out of the teenagers. Each team will grip the end of a rope as they stand facing one another.

Tell the teenagers to grasp the rope firmly. The group moderator will sound the whistle when all the teams are prepared.

To bring down the other team, the teams begin tugging on the ropes with all their might and planning. The winner of the game is the team that successfully pushes the other team across the center line.

24. "Tower of Hanoi"

A puzzle toy with three towers or pegs is required. At the very end, one tower will be made up of numerous discs, with the biggest on the bottom and the smallest on top.

Moving the complete stack of discs from one tower to the other end is the objective.

While moving pegs to the other end, the team can temporarily assemble the pegs in the middle tower. The only restrictions are that you can only move one disc at once and can't stack bigger discs on smaller ones.

The game has a clock. The winning team is the one that successfully moves every disc from one tower to the next. The game has logical and mathematical twists that provide plenty of chances for conversation, planning, and problem-solving.

25. The exercise in consensus.

Divide them into four or more teams depending on the players' strengths. Each team must congregate together and prepare a sound and action to execute for the other teams at the mediator's signal.

For the other teams, each team performs twice. Each team aims to produce the same sound and do the same action simultaneously. The game will go on until every group synchronizes their sounds and motions.

26. Cross the hula loop.

Make the participants line up while one child holds a hula loop stick in his hand.

Instruct the participants to link hands to attempt the shuffle, push, and shimmy together. To transfer the hula loop to the partner next to them, they must shuffle it over their shoulders, arms, and legs.

The objective is to cross the loop completely without severing the chain. Any player who drops the loop will join the team. The winning team is the one that can move the hula hoop from one end to the other in the least amount of time.

27. Helium stick

The participants should form two squads and line up shoulder to shoulder. Each participant raises their hands in front of them with his palms facing up.

They interlace their fingers, pointing only the index finger in front. Please set up a long rod so that each player's finger is resting on it.

The team members have to set the rod on the ground or floor without dropping it when the count is three. The winning team is the one that completes the task first or in the quickest time.

How to Maintain Teams' Interest during the Team-building Exercise

Use these suggestions to get teen boys involved and keep them interested.

- Pick games with simple goals that you can understand and complete.
- You may make the goals challenging while yet making sure it is doable.
- Teens may lose motivation and stop participating actively if a goal appears unreachable.
- Explain the advantages of the proposed activity in plain language.
- Create a reward system to foster a competitive and enthusiastic atmosphere.
- Make the task appealing and challenging. For instance, placing obstacles on the racing course might make a straightforward run difficult.
- Establish a climate of collaboration and trust in your role as a trainer, mediator, or facilitator.

- During the activity, lead and inspire them and work to maintain their spirits.
- Explain the activity's safety precautions and guidelines in detail.
- Even if you have taken steps to ensure participant safety, keep an eye out while playing or participating in the activity.
- Set appropriate sanctions for disregarding limits and safety regulations.

Team-building exercises promote teamwork, excellent planning abilities, and improved communication. It fosters trust, builds problem-solving skills, and enhances sportsmanship and collaboration.

Teens may organize these easy events at gatherings and schools.

You may modify them as well based on the preferences and size of the group. Take photographs and record films of yourself when you engage in these activities so you may look back on these experiences in the future.

How to Practice Responsible Decision Making is next in Chapter 5. Happy Reading.

CHAPTER 5

PRACTICE RESPONSIBLE DECISION MAKING

Nobody has unique decision-making abilities from birth. It's a great skill that must be developed but may never be fully mastered. It implies that the more choices you make, the better you will get at them.

It's a challenging skill to master, however, since the more adept you get at making decisions, the more complex challenges you'll encounter. Some individuals experience anxiety while making decisions, worrying that they will choose poorly.

Any time you have a choice between two options, there is always a possibility that you will choose the "better" or "worse" option. Although you can anticipate where each choice will lead you, you frequently won't know how wise your choice was until some time has passed.

Choosing a college or university, moving out on your own, getting a job, or just concentrating on school, determining if your friends are genuine, or deciding whether or not to notify others of bullying or a crime you witnessed usually requires more thought than simpler decisions.

Remember that many decisions you'll need to make don't have a right or incorrect solution. It would be best if you thus decided based on what you understand about yourself, your circumstances, your requirements, and your goals, as well as what you believe would be best for you.

Making decisions has an impact on daily living, and over time, we pick up these abilities from those around us. Teen boys require parental guidance to establish sound decision-making practices since they tend to make snap decisions early in life.

Making decisions involves more than just making a decision. It involves figuring out what has to be done, how to execute it, and thinking back on the reasons why and the results.

When someone has strong decision-making skills, they recognize why certain activities are better for their welfare and the well-being of others, and they have adequate expectations regarding what their acts (or lack of it) will do.

When a person uses healthy decision-making, they can see when they're responding impulsively and the possible causes of those sentiments. They will also be able to assess future outcomes in hopes of getting better ones.

Understanding the Decision-making Process

Teenagers should work on developing this talent since it will enable them to make wise and responsible decisions.

Recognizing an issue or circumstance, obtaining data, weighing choices, making a decision, and acting are all steps in the decision-making process.

The Importance of Practicing Responsible Decision Making

1. Help to understand the repercussions of actions.

Children must comprehend the effects of their actions. They initially discover this when they scream for food. Still, to develop into compassionate, responsible adults, they must understand how and why their actions influence themselves and others.

They may not get what they want out of choice, or what they desire might not be the wisest course of action, so teen boys should utilize errors as teaching opportunities and link repercussions to well-being.

2. Helps them develop foresight.

Once they comprehend the repercussions, they can see how decisions affect the bigger picture—their future. They might discover how decisions made for immediate enjoyment may not take into account what is ultimately crucial.

A goal inspires motivation and gives lesser choices meaning. Setting a realistic goal on what you enjoy can help you maintain your patience while you wait for success, which may be difficult.

3. Leave a lasting impression.

People who engage in long-term life planning give themselves a greater number of possibilities to plan for successful outcomes. You will comprehend how decision-making has a wider impact on individuals and their communities as you become more aware of how your actions influence your future.

4. Gives them confidence and empowers them.

Teenagers discover the true significance of their views when actions have tangible effects on their life. It is empowering for people to realize that their opinions matter. It serves as an inspiration to continue making wise decisions.

Teen boys adept at making responsible decisions have the freedom to choose actions that will help them develop.

How to Develop Responsible Decision Making

1. What issue are you dealing with?

Concentrating on your studies or working a part-time job, for instance? First, to be certain of your goals, write them in writing. List the reasons you should resolve this problem.

For instance

- What are your priorities? You can see from this stage how crucial this decision is.

2. Collect information.

- Request guidance.
- Whatever you need to learn, please put it in writing.
- Talk to people: Parents, friends, family, teacher, etc
- What are the opinions of those who have previously experienced this?
- Obtain facts from reliable sources. For instance, ask your school counselor how many hours per week a part-time work requires against how many hours/per week school requires.
- Which facts apply?
- What is preventing you? For instance, poor habits, a dread of responsibility, or the idea that you can't manage both.

This stage provides objective (unbiased) and subjective (biased) data.

3. What matters to you?

- Describe your values—for instance, integrity, success in school, wealth, independence, etc.
- Which circumstances do you want your decision to reflect?
- What is your family's viewpoint?

4. Generate ideas and list potential solutions.

- Create options and ideas that you can choose from.

Work 5 hours, 9 hours, don't work, only work during the summer, etc.

5. What are the results (positive and negative) of each decision?

To weigh the advantages and disadvantages of each option provided in step 4, you may use stages 2 and 3. To have all the facts in front of you, write things down in a journal.

6. Select the one that is ideal for you.

.After you complete the steps mentioned earlier, this becomes much simpler. Rank your decisions, if necessary.

Rank the items in order using your research. If you need to, take some days to reflect before returning to the problem.

7. Make a plan and follow it.

Once you've decided, make a plan outlining the precise actions you'll take and execute your strategy.

8. Calculate the outcomes.

You can only do this once you've made a decision, followed through on your strategy, and get some feedback.

For example, your school result and academic performance.

- What would you say about your decisions?
- How did the actions you took go?
- Are you still fulfilling your priorities?
- What lessons have you taken away?

It is a crucial action for improving your ability to make decisions. Use everything you've learned to return to the drawing board and reassess your decision if you realize it didn't turn out well the first time.

It would not be the end of the game if the first decision weren't the best. Backtrack your steps and begin at the finest location you can

9. Consult an expert

A second opinion might help you feel more confident about your decisions and legitimize your conclusions.

You can talk to your parents, consult a reliable friend or attempt to find a local authority. You may ask your teacher what they think of the assignment you're working on.

10. Keep everything in context.

Consider evaluating the worth of each decision.

Focus on more significant issues, like studying and completing a vital math textbook, rather than discussing minor ones, like the font style of the book. You may learn to be more adaptable and able to compromise by keeping each decision in perspective.

11. Set due dates.

Set time limits for yourself while making each decision, which may reduce the time you need to decide or alter your opinion.

You should gauge the significance of your decision first. If it could have a significant effect, you might need more time to consider, which might help you become better at managing your time.

12. Be selective

The more options you have, the more difficult it is to make a decision. By reducing your alternatives, you may make a decision after carefully weighing a smaller number of them.

Having fewer options teaches you to think when evaluating the alternatives that are still available. For instance, concentrate on photographs that express your class's narrative easily when picking an image for your class's social media account and exclude those does not fit.

13. Evaluate your choices.

Consider compiling a list of each choice's advantages and disadvantages, and it will assist you in making an educated assessment of all your alternatives and choices.

You could even come up with new things to ponder about as a result. You may examine your decisions more honestly and in an organized manner by listing all the benefits and drawbacks. It will benefit your ability to think critically, analyze situations, and solve problems.

14. Exercise

Since it assists in stimulating your brain and increases your energy levels, physical activity can help your mind and body work together. Additionally, it may enhance your capacity for decision-making.

15. Make new pals

Having a diverse group of contacts may open your eyes to new ideas and provide you with insightful counsel while making decisions. Working with new colleagues and friends may develop your collaboration and active listening abilities.

You may ask your friends and colleagues how to handle a particular issue with a project.

Some people may not have encountered that issue, while others might have. You have more individuals to turn to for assistance or dependable counsel if you have more friends and acquaintances.

16. Conduct experiments

You may use experiments to test your judgments using scientific models. Create an experiment comparable to your decision if you need clarification about the outcome or course of action.

You may construct your experiment procedures using strategy and study to anticipate a hypothesis.

17. Practice

Making responsible decisions repeatedly might train your brain to make decisions more rapidly when the situation demands it.

In the next you will learn how to Develop Resilience.

YOUR OPINION MATTERS

Hello and thank you for choosing to read this book! I hope you're getting lots of value as you read through.

As an author, it means a lot to me to hear feedback from my readers. Your reviews are incredibly important to me as they help reach new readers and just a few sentences can go a long way.

By leaving a review, you will be providing valuable insight and information to others seeking the exact information shared in this book.

By taking the time to leave a review, you are contributing to the online community of readers who share similar interests and concerns. Your review can spark conversations and inspire others to share their own thoughts and experiences.

If you have a few moments to spare, I would greatly appreciate it if you could leave a review of this book on Amazon.

Your support means the world to me and helps me to continue researching and creating great books that provide value for readers like you.

Scan the ***QR code*** below to leave a review

CHAPTER 6

DEVELOP RESILIENCE

For young people, it is crucial to have the capacity to adjust successfully to challenging circumstances. The bright side is that developing resilience is a learnable ability.

Television and social make growing up seem so simple; everyone looks like they are having fun, hanging out with their buddies, and dressing appropriately. However, if you're an adolescent, you are aware of how difficult life can be at times. Bullying to the passing of a parent or acquaintance is just a few of the issues you could experience.

Why is it that specific individuals can go through such difficult situations and yet recover? The distinction is that individuals who recover do so by exercising resilience.

The best part is that you can gain resilience abilities; they are not something you either have or don't. Some individuals seem to have "bounce," whilst others don't, due to resilience, which is the capacity to adapt successfully in the face of adversity, such as difficult circumstances, catastrophes such as earthquakes, hurricanes, fires, dangers, or even severe stress.

The ease with which you can handle and recover from life's challenges is known as resilience. It may mean the distinction between keeping your composure under pressure and losing it.

Resilient people keep a more upbeat attitude and handle stress better.

Research has revealed that although resilience may appear to come quickly to certain individuals, it is also possible to acquire these characteristics. Building resilience is essential whether or not you're currently going through a difficult period or want to be ready for problems in the future.

The Seven Pillars of Resilience.

You must comprehend the 7 C's of resilience before I provide you with the practical techniques to support your development of resilience.

- **Confidence**

Confident young individuals will believe that they will eventually achieve and will be more inclined to take the risks necessary to understand themselves. They could be more motivated to succeed and less afraid of failing.

More importantly, they'll bounce back from failure, viewing it as a chance for development rather than a disaster.

- **Competence**

For teen boys to be equipped to survive in the world, they need to have practical skill sets. These include:

- ✓ Academic skills
- ✓ Peer negotiation and conflict resolution skills
- ✓ Self-advocacy skills
- ✓ And communication skills

If teen boys want to make the kinds of decisions that will benefit rather than harm their health and well-being, they additionally require to be able to make responsible decisions.

- **Connection**

The human connection enables us to rejoice more thoroughly during happy occasions and heal through difficult ones.

The most protective factor in your life is your relationship with people, founded on your understanding of who you are. Hopefully, you will establish this protective relationship in addition to many others. More is always better.

- **Character**

Young individuals who have solid fundamental beliefs are more likely to make significant contributions, feel more confident about themselves, and form stable, loving relationships.

Consider character traits as those qualities that guarantee we conduct ourselves morally even when no one is looking. People with moral integrity are what the world needs.

- **Contribution**

Teens want significance. They want to live lives that are meaningful and purposeful in the end. Giving teenagers a chance to change the world also gives them powerful self-defense mechanisms.

They experience the delight of giving personally. It finally implies that individuals may get help from others without feeling guilty. Why? They'll realize that the individual standing by them is doing it out of compassion rather than sympathy.

They receive appreciation through making a difference in other people's lives. Young people flourish in an environment that values gratitude above censure.

- **Coping**

Making decisions is a part of life, and stress is an unpleasant reality that is also part of life. We make every effort to reduce stress, and we may choose to deal with our stress in either a good or bad way.

Negative ones may be effective in the short term but cause enormous long-term damage to ourselves and society. Resilience gives us the capacity to cope with stress.

- **Control**

Understanding that your activities matter is essential to resilience. We are unable to feel hopeful without a feeling of control, and in trying times, we crumble without hope.

How to Become More Resilient

1. Discover Your Purpose.

You may discover meaning in life's adversities by developing a sense of purpose. With a clear goal, you won't let your challenges demotivate you; instead, you'll be more inspired to draw lessons from the past and continue.

Examples of purposes are as follows:

- Assembling a network of close friends and family.
- Giving a social movement a voice.
- Maintaining a fit lifestyle.
- Studying various cultural traditions.
- Creating music or art.
- Serving your neighborhood

Developing a sense of purpose may be particularly crucial to your rehabilitation when dealing with emotional adversity, such as the loss of a family member or the breakdown of a relationship. Getting active in your community, developing your faith, or participating in pursuits that are personally significant to you.

2. Have faith in your skills.

Resilience may greatly benefit from faith in one's capacity to handle life's hardships. An excellent method to develop resilience for the future is to become more confident in your skills, particularly your capacity to react to and handle a crisis.

Keep an ear out for critical thoughts in your brain. Practice replacing negative thoughts with positive ones as soon as you hear them, such as "I can do this," "I'm a great friend," or "I'm good at my work."

According to research, self-esteem is crucial for managing stress and returning from traumatic experiences.

3. Establish a robust network of support

It's essential to have trustworthy friends and family. Having a kind, encouraging individuals close by may be a calming influence in trying circumstances.

While discussing a problem with other people or loved ones is unlikely to make your problems disappear, it allows you to express your feelings, acquire support, get good advice, and think of potential solutions.

4. Accept change

Resilience depends heavily on flexibility. If you learn to be more flexible, you'll be better prepared to react when a crisis occurs.

Resilient people frequently take advantage of these situations to explore new opportunities. While sudden changes can be devastating to some people, highly resilient people are able to adjust and thrive.

5. Positivity

While maintaining a positive outlook in difficult times can be challenging, resilience heavily relies on optimism. Even if what you are going through may be hard, it's crucial to have optimism and hope for a better future.

Neglecting the issue in favor of concentrating on the good does not constitute positive thinking. It entails realizing that setbacks are transient and that you have the knowledge, tools, and resources necessary to overcome the difficulties you encounter.

6. Look after yourself

It's effortless to put off taking care of your personal needs when you're under stress. Common responses to a crisis scenario include losing your appetite, skipping exercise, and not having enough sleep. Instead, concentrate on developing your ability to care for yourself even while you're struggling.

Make time for the things you like doing. You may improve your general health and resilience and be completely prepared to tackle life's difficulties by taking care of your personal needs.

7. Master problem-solving techniques

According to research, persons who have the capacity to solve difficulties have a tendency to handle stress more effectively than those who are unable to do so.

Make a short list of possible solutions whenever you face a new obstacle. Try out several approaches and concentrate on coming up with a logical solution to frequent issues.

Regularly exercising your problem-solving abilities will make you more equipped to handle difficult situations.

8. Set goals

Situations of crisis are frightening. They could seem impossible. People, via resilience, are able to approach these situations realistically and then establish practical goals to address the issue.

Take one step back to quickly evaluate the issue if you find yourself feeling overpowered by it. Create a list of potential solutions and then divide them into actionable stages.

9. Do something

Simply hoping that a problem will go away on its own will only make it worse. Instead, go to work on fixing the problem right away. You may take action to improve your circumstances and reduce stress, even if there might not be a quick or easy fix.

Instead of being overwhelmed by the quantity of work that requires to be done, concentrate on the progress you have achieved so far and prepare for your future steps. You'll feel greater in control if you actively pursue solutions.

Being proactive enables you to contribute to the realization of your goals instead of just waiting for them to occur.

10. Continue honing your skills.

Don't give up if you still struggle to deal with difficult occurrences since resilience may take time to develop. Being resilient is a skill everyone can acquire, and it doesn't need particular behaviors or acts.

People's levels of resilience may differ significantly from one another. Focus on developing these abilities and the traits that resilient individuals share, but keep in mind to capitalize on your current assets.

11. Be kind to yourself.

When something negative occurs in your life, the emotional strain you are already experiencing may become worse. Hormones and bodily changes may have already caused your emotions to be all over the place, but the uncertainty that comes with anguish or trauma may make these changes feel much more dramatic. Be ready for this and be kind to yourself.

12. Establish a hassle-free area.

Create a "hassle-free zone" in your room or apartment; you don't have to barricade yourself in, but there should be no tension or worries. However, be aware that if a significant event has recently occurred, your siblings and parents may be experiencing stress and might like to spend more time with you than usual.

13. Adhere to the plan.

Try to remain consistent since being in high school or on a university campus implies having more options. Plan a schedule and follow it while under a lot of stress.

Keep up with the routines that bring you comfort, whether things you do before class, heading out to lunch, or calling a buddy every night. You may be trying a lot of new things.

14. Rest and sleep well.

Make sure to look after your physical, mental, and spiritual well-being by resting and sleeping well. If you don't, you could become more tense and impatient when you need to maintain your composure.

There's a great deal going on, and it will be challenging to deal with if you keep nodding off while standing.

15. Exercise command.

You may progress toward your goals by taking baby steps even when tragedy or extreme uncertainty is present. Even if all you can do at a particularly trying period is get out of bed as well as go to school, doing so may be beneficial.

Consider what you have control over and what is out of your control but something you can change. We often feel out of control when things are bad; regain some of that control by acting decisively.

16. Express your feelings.

Tragic events and substantial problems may trigger a range of contradictory feelings, but there are times when it's simply too difficult to express them to others. If talking doesn't help, try writing in a notebook or doing art to express your feelings.

17. Assist someone.

Nothing helps you focus on addressing other people's issues more than your own.

Try cleaning up around your home or apartment, doing some community or school volunteer work, or assisting a friend with their schoolwork in person or online. Consider the bigger picture. Everyone may be discussing the same subject that's making you anxious.

However, things do turn around, and bad times pass. If you're unsure of your ability to go past this, consider a moment when you overcame your reservations, such as when you applied for a job or asked for a date. Learn some relaxing strategies, such as picturing a serene setting, thinking about certain music when stressed, or just breathing a few deep breaths to help you unwind.

Consider the important items that haven't changed despite the outer world's changes, and discuss both good and bad times whenever you talk about difficult times.

18. Disconnect

You want to be informed; perhaps your schoolwork involves watching the news.

But occasionally, the news can exacerbate the impression that everything needs to be fixed because it emphasizes the sensational. Try to minimize the quantity of info you consume, whether from the internet, Television, newspapers, or magazines.

Some news stories are sensational; viewing them again increases tension and provides no new information.

Note: You can develop resilience, but even if you develop resilience, you could still experience stress or anxiety. It's okay if there are instances when you're not happy.

Each individual will go at their own pace on the road of resilience. Some of the resilience, as mentioned earlier advice may help you, while others may help some of your friends.

It is a good idea to have these resilience-building skills on a daily basis since they will be helpful long after the difficult times have passed. You may become one of those folks who "get bounced" by having resilience.

Learn how to Manage Stress through Relaxation Techniques in Chapter 7. See you there

CHAPTER 7

LEARN HOW TO MANAGE STRESS THROUGH RELAXATION TECHNIQUES

Life is complicated. Let's face it. Some aspects of everyday life are tedious, infuriating, and unpleasant regardless of age, whether you're an adolescent, an adult, or an older adult.

Additionally, some seasons and times of year of life are more stressful for all of us than others. Stress may be short-term, like a few months of joblessness, or long-term, like a persistent medical condition.

Teen boys must balance the demands of school, work, friends, and domestic chores with the enormous task of becoming mature and independent. Gaining the ability to relax significantly improves your quality of life.

Teenagers now experience more worry and stress than any previous generation, so they must thus learn how to relax. And techniques for relaxation provide profitable strategies to manage stress.

With relaxation techniques, they have a greater chance of avoiding negative coping strategies like drug misuse and self-harm.

Many associate relaxation with chilling out in front of the Television on the sofa after a demanding day. However, it doesn't do much to lessen the negative effects of stress.

Instead, you should trigger your body's natural relaxation reaction, a deep sleep-like condition that reduces stress, relaxes your heart and breathing rate, and blood pressure, and restores harmony to your body and mind.

You may engage in relaxation exercises like yoga, tai chi, deep breathing, meditation, and rhythmic movement.

Throughout our lives, we will encounter stressful situations ranging from small inconveniences like congestion to more severe concerns, like a loved one's serious illness.

Stress releases a barrage of hormones into your body, regardless of the source. Your respiration quickens, your muscles stiffen up, and your heart pounds.

This so-called "stress response" is a typical response to dangerous circumstances that evolved during our prehistoric ancestors' survival of hazards like animal attacks and floods. Although we no longer frequently encounter these physical threats, stressful circumstances in everyday life can still trigger the stress response.

We can't and can't eliminate stress from our lives. But we can find better ways to react to them. And managing stress by utilizing relaxation methods is helpful.

How to Manage Stress through Relaxation Techniques

1. Deep breathing

Deep breathing, which emphasizes taking long, cleansing breaths, is a simple yet effective relaxing method. It offers a rapid technique to reduce stress levels and is simple to learn and perform practically any place.

The foundation of many different methods of relaxation is deep breathing, which you may combine with other calming habits like aromatherapy and music. While you can follow along with apps and audio downloads, all you require is a few minutes and a peaceful spot to sit or stretch out.

How to do deep breathing exercises

- With your back straight, choose a comfortable seat.
- Hold your tummy with one hand and your chest with the other.
- Breathe via your nose.
- As you exhale, contract your abdominal muscles and force as much air as you can out of your mouth.
- When you exhale, your other hand should barely move, and your hand on the belly should move in.
- Breathe through your nose and out via your mouth as you normally would.
- Make an effort to take in enough air so your lower belly rises and falls.
- Slowly count as you exhale.

- Try reclining down if you have trouble breathing from your belly when standing up.
- Put a tiny book on your tummy and breathe such that it rises and falls with each inhalation and exhalation.

2: Progressive muscle relaxation

In a two-step procedure known as progressive muscle relaxation, various body muscular groups are sequentially strained and relaxed. Regular practice enables you to get intimately aware of how different sections of your body feel under strain as well as when they are completely relaxed.

It might assist you in responding to the earliest indications of stress-related physical tension. Additionally, your mind will unwind as your body does. Deep breathing and progressive muscular relaxation may be used together to relax and reduce stress further.

How to do Progression of muscular relaxation.

If you have a track record of back issues, muscular spasms, or other severe ailments that might be made worse by tensing your muscles, talk to your doctor first.

- Working your way up to your face from your feet, try to focus just on tensing the correct muscles.
- Get comfortable by loosening your clothes and taking off your shoes.
- Spend a few minutes taking calm, deep breaths in and out.

- Turn your focus to your right foot when you're prepared to do so.
- Spend a minute concentrating on the sensation.
- Squeeze your right foot's muscles as firmly as you can while gradually tensing them.
- Hold for ten counts.
- Your foot will feel relaxed. Please pay attention to how your foot is feeling as it turns limp and free as the tension leaves it.
- For a minute, remain in this calm condition while taking slow, deep breaths.
- Turn your focus to your left foot.
- Maintain the same pattern of tension and relaxation in your muscles.
- Contract and relax the various muscle groups as you gently go up your body.
- Try not to tighten any muscles other than the ones you need to. It could take some getting used to at first.

3: Mindfulness of the body scan

This kind of meditation directs your attention to different areas of your body. Like progressive muscle relaxation, you begin at your feet and work your way up. You concentrate on how each area of your body feels without categorizing the feelings as "good" or "bad" rather than tensing and relaxing your muscles.

- Lay on your back with your legs straight, your arms at your sides, and your eyes open or closed.
- Spend roughly two minutes concentrating on your breathing to begin to relax.

- Pay attention to your right foot's toes now.
- While keeping your attention on your breathing, pay attention to any feelings you experience.
- Each deep inhale should travel to your toes.
- Keep your
- Attention on this spot for three to five seconds or longer.
- Pay attention to any bodily sensations you experience there, and visualize each breath coming from the bottom of your foot.
- After a few seconds, shift your attention to your right ankle and continue.
- It would be best if you now moved to your calf, knee, thigh, and hip. Repeat this motion with your left leg.

Start at the lower back and abdomen and work up the torso, passing through the upper back and chest, then the shoulders. Pay particular attention to any body part that is bothering you or giving you pain.

After finishing the body scan, take some time to unwind in solitude and quiet while observing how your body is feeling. After then, gently open your eyes and move if needed.

4: Visualization

In visualization, also known as guided imagery, you imagine a peaceful setting where you are free to let go of all anxiety and stress. It is a variance in traditional meditation. Pick a location that makes you feel at ease, whether or not it's a tropical beach, a place you loved as a child or a peaceful wooded area.

You may use an application or audio download to help you with your visualization exercises, or you can practice independently. You may also decide to execute your visualization in complete quiet or with the use of listening aids, such as calming music, a sound machine, or a recording that corresponds to your selected location, such as the sound of waves on a beach.

Practicing visualization

- Imagine your peaceful location while you close your eyes.
- Imagine everything in as much detail as you can, including everything you hear, taste, smell, and feel.
- It is not sufficient to "look" at it in your subconscious mind as you would a picture. The finest visualization results come from as many sensory elements as you can.

For instance, suppose you were considering building a pier on a serene lake:

- Watch the sunset over the lake.
- Hear the song of the birds singing
- The fragrance of the pine trees
- Feel the refreshing water on your naked feet.
- Since the pure, fresh air.

As you carefully explore your peaceful location, savor the sensation of your worries fading away. Open your eyes slowly when you're ready and focus on the moment. It's normal sometimes to lose track of where you are or zone out while on a visualization session. That is typical. Yawning, muscular twitching, and stiffness in your limbs are some possible symptoms.

5. Self-massaging.

You are undoubtedly well aware of the significant benefits of an expert massage at a spa or fitness center on lowering stress, easing pain, and easing muscular tension. You may not know that you can get some of the same advantages at home by self-massaging or exchanging messages with loved ones.

Try giving yourself a little massage on the sofa after a long day or in bed to assist you in relaxing before night. You may use scented lotion or fragrant oils to promote relaxation or mix self-talk with mindfulness or deep breathing exercises.

A five-minute stress-relieving self-massage.

- For best results, combine your strokes to loosen up your muscles.
- Use your hands edges as soft chops, or tap with your fingers or palms cupped.
- Apply fingertip pressure to any knotted muscles.
- Knead over the muscles while attempting long, gentle strokes.
- Any body part that is within ease can receive these strokes.
- Try concentrating on the neck and head for a little session like this
- Start by massaging the back of your neck along with your shoulders your muscles.
- Make a loose fist and quickly rub the back and sides of your neck with it.
- Next, make little circles with your thumbs around the base of your skull.

- With your fingertips, gently massage the remaining portion of your scalp.
- Next, tap your scalp with your fingers as you move them over the sides, back, and front.

Face massage.

- A combination of your thumbs or fingertips makes a string of tiny circles.
- Pay close attention to the muscles in your jaw, forehead, and temples.
- Start by massaging your nasal bridge with your middle fingers, then go outward along your brows and to your temples.
- Lastly, shut your eyes. For a little while, breathe in and out comfortably while cupping your hands gently over your face.

6: Mindfulness

In recent years, mindfulness has gained enormous popularity, receiving press coverage and support from celebrities, corporate titans, and psychiatrists alike.

And what exactly is mindfulness?

By shifting your attention to what is occurring right now, mindfulness enables you to be completely present rather than stressing about the future or obsessing over the past.

Reduced stress, anxiety, despair, and other unpleasant emotions are expected outcomes of mindfulness-based meditation practices. By concentrating your attention on just one repeating activity, like your breathing or some repeated phrases, several techniques help you become more present.

Some mindfulness practices encourage attention and letting go of internal emotions or sensations. Exercise, eating, and other activities may all benefit from practicing mindfulness.

Practicing mindfulness to keep your attention in the present may seem simple, but it takes effort to benefit from it. When you begin to practice, you'll notice that your thoughts often return to your concerns or regrets.

Don't give up, however. You're developing a new mental attitude that might aid you in letting go of worrying about past experiences or the future every time you bring your attention back to the present. When you're starting, employing an application or audio download may also help you concentrate.

A simple mindfulness exercise

- Locate a peaceful area free from distractions and interruptions.
- A comfy chair should have a straight back.
- You may use your breathing, the feeling of air moving into and out of your mouth, or the rise and fall of your stomach as a point of attention. You can even repeat a meaningful phrase during the meditation.
- Don't be concerned about your performance or the distracting ideas running through your head.
- If thoughts interrupt your relaxation, don't fight them; instead, gently and without condemnation, bring your focus back to the thing you were concentrating on.

7: Rhythmic exercise and conscious movement.

Although exercising may not seem mostly relaxing, rhythmic exercise that induces continuous motion flow can cause a relaxation response.

Examples are:

- Running
- Walking
- Swimming
- Dancing
- Rowing
- Climbing

Even though rhythmic exercise alone can help you reduce stress, incorporating mindfulness can have even more significant advantages. To participate in mindful exercise, you must be present and focused on your body's current sensations rather than on everyday problems or anxieties.

Concentrate on the feelings in your limbs and how your breathing accompanies your movement while you exercise rather than drifting off or glancing at the TV.

Consider concentrating on the feeling of your feet contacting the ground when you're walking or jogging, your breathing pattern, and the sensation of the wind hitting your face.

Focus on breathing in time with your movements throughout resistance training, and concentrate on how your body reacts as you raise and decrease the weights. And when your thoughts stray, gently bring them back to your breathing and motion.

8: Tai chi and yoga.

Yoga involves a sequence of dynamic and still positions and deep breathing. Yoga may help with strength, flexibility, balance, endurance, anxiety, and tension.

Yoga injuries may result from improper technique. Therefore, learning by enrolling in group courses, paying for a private instructor, or watching instructional videos is better. Once you've mastered the fundamentals, you can practice by yourself or with other people, customizing your practice as necessary.

What kind of yoga relieves the stress the best?

Although almost all yoga classes conclude with a relaxation pose, the most effective classes for de-stressing focus on slow, constant motion, deep breathing, and easy stretching.

- **Satyananda.**

One kind of classical yoga is Satyananda. It is appropriate for novices as well as anybody looking to reduce stress since it includes gentle postures, deep relaxation, and meditation.

- **Hatha yoga**

Hatha yoga is also a beginner-friendly, somewhat mild form of stress relief. When choosing a yoga class, look for designations like gentle, stress reduction, or beginners. With its challenging postures and emphasis on fitness, Hatha yoga is more suitable for people seeking stimulation and relaxation.

Tai chi

You've probably seen tai chi if you've ever seen a group of individuals moving slowly and in unison in a park. Tai chi is a gentle, fluid set of motions performed at your speed.

You may maintain your attention in the present by concentrating on your breathing and movements, which helps to cleanse your mind and put you in a calm condition. Everyone of a variety of ages and fitness levels, even older persons and those recuperating from injuries may practice tai chi since it is a secure, low-impact activity.

Like yoga, it is best learned in class or from a private teacher. After mastering the fundamentals, you may practice alone or with others.

Although it's simple to pick up the fundamentals of these relaxation techniques, consistent practice is necessary to unlock their stress-relieving potential fully. Consider scheduling at least 10 to 20 minutes every day for relaxing.

Schedule some time in your day. Plan to practice a few times a day at a certain time. If you already have a full schedule, consider doing some meditation while riding the bus or train to work, having a yoga or tai chi break over lunch, or engaging in mindful walking while walking your dog.

Make advantage of tools such as smartphone applications. Numerous individuals discover that smartphone applications or audio downloads can be helpful in instructing them through various relaxation techniques, creating a routine, and monitoring progress.

Expect both highs and lows. The full benefits of relaxing methods like meditation may require time and practice. The longer you persevere, the quicker you'll see benefits. Keep going if you miss some days or a few weeks at a time. Start over and gradually gather your previous momentum.

Learn how to Develop Good Critical thinking Skills in the next Chapter. Happy Reading.

CHAPTER 8

DEVELOP GOOD CRITICAL THINKING SKILLS

One of the main issues with teens is their need for critical thinking skills. Schools need to do more to help pupils improve their critical thinking skills.

These abilities are crucial, which is why we want to examine them with you. It might seem unimportant for success, but it is quite the opposite.

Teenagers need a basic understanding of critical thinking skills and are unsure of the advantages critical thinking abilities may bring to their life.

Making sensible decisions that are well-thought-out and rational requires critical thinking skills.

As a teen boy, you shouldn't believe every justification and conclusion you hear. It would be best if you made an effort to investigate everything thoroughly, ask the necessary questions, and then come to your findings and reasons.

You must first determine the skills critical thinking entails to learn how to improve them.

What exactly are "Critical Thinking Skills"?

Critical thinking skills include:

1. Analytical
2. Communication
3. Creativity
4. Open-Minded
5. Problem-solving

I'll categorize these critical thinking skills as "subskills." It will help you understand what "critical thinking skills" are.

1. **Analytical**

All of the pieces of information that you receives has to be carefully considered. There is a good risk that you will draw incorrect conclusions if you do not comprehend the facts you get.

Here are a few illustrations of this group of critical thinking skills:

- Analysis of Data
- Searching for information
- Posing "useful" inquiries
- Decision
- Identifying contrasts and parallels, etc.

2. **Communication**

Teens often need to gain an understanding of what good communication skills are. Verbal, nonverbal, and written communication all fall under this category of critical thinking skills, and you can only properly develop critical thinking skills if you work on each one individually. It's crucial that you don't omit any of them.

Here are some types of effective communication:

- Explanation
- Collaboration
- Presentation
- Teamwork
- Written communication (such as networking)
- Personality traits, etc.

3. **Creativity**

Creativity is a vital component of critical thinking skills. Remember that certain information will be available to you later. Because of this, you sometimes need to make predictions and consider what might occur if you take a certain action.

Here are some examples of creativity:

- Curiosity
- Imagination
- Predicting
- Synthesizing
- Concept development, etc.

4. Open-Minded

Being impartial is challenging. Every teen will have the chance to discover that.

Suppose your mind is not receptive to it. In that case, it is impossible to develop critical thinking abilities, and you won't be able to properly assess the information you get if your mind is "closed." Being open-minded means that you can:

- Inclusive
- Fair
- Observation
- Reflection
- Humble

5. Problem-solving

The dread of uncertainty is one of the key reasons young people want to avoid starting their businesses. They find it difficult to deal with stress and common issues.

Problem-solving is another essential cognitive ability that kids must develop because of this. You may learn to build critical thinking skills by overcoming your anxieties and concentrating on the answer.

The following are the things you should possess and enhance:

- Observation of details
- Clarification
- Decision-making

- Innovative abilities
- Setting goals, etc.

Now that you are aware of what critical thinking skills are, it is appropriate to look at how to acquire them. Do not anticipate your critical thinking skills will be flawless by tomorrow since the process takes time and patience.

Developing Critical Thinking Skills

You may learn how to increase critical thinking skills by following a number of different stages.

To be more exact, you must complete different stages in order to reach your objective:

- Ask important and meaningful questions
- Consider what you hear
- Determine Information Sources
- Continually conduct research
- Self-examination
- Build on your strengths while improving your weaknesses
- Make it Simple

Let's discuss ways to improve your critical thinking skills.

1. Ask Important and meaningful questions.

You are well aware of how crucial it is to educate oneself on useful knowledge. However, those details won't appear on their own.

It would be best if you searched for them, but you need to ask good questions. It will be inefficient to ask and look into the incorrect subjects because finding accurate and worthwhile bits of information is a must for developing critical thinking skills.

Many teen boys have access to a wealth of knowledge. But will every piece of information you get help you hone your critical-thinking skills?

A useful resource for getting the information you need is Internet technology. You may learn a lot from a variety of useful blogs, vlogs, electronic books, and other educational resources to improve. These are the venues where accomplished, educated, and experienced individuals discuss their life and professional experiences.

2. Consider what you hear

You should carefully consider what you hear. You sometimes get excellent knowledge when you acquire bits of it.

Consider the scenario where you wish to buy a new device. You may need more professional and personal experience. You'll naturally start to inquire about the company.

You do not have to agree with everything you hear, though. It would be best if you recorded your recommendations on paper. Read them attentively and consider what might occur if you followed other people's advice.

It is the time to apply your critical thinking skills. Consider everything and evaluate everything. Use your imagination to see the precise outcome of your choice or conclusion.

Though you might make mistakes at first, don't let them scare you. Remember that the finest lessons you can learn are through your failures. Even successful people with experience make mistakes.

3. Determine Information Sources

We've previously shown that only some viewpoints or finding that we get are constructive.

But a lot depends on the origin of the information you receive in terms of its quality. Different sources may have provided this data. For instance, we may ask our parents, relatives, and friends for guidance.

It may also take the shape of a podcast, video, article, or book. You must first identify the source of the information before you can begin to listen.

You'll need to use your critical thinking skills to qualify this information. Assume for a moment that you want a mentor. The majority of young people need more ability to distinguish between excellent ones. They believe that years of expertise should be the key factor to consider.

A real mentor combines education, life experience, and a desire to assist others in bettering their circumstances. To assist you, he must comprehend your situation and sentiments. For this reason, if you're serious about honing your critical thinking skills, you must first identify your information's source.

4. Continually conduct research

Your commitment and effort will greatly affect how well you develop critical thinking skills. As we just said, you need to investigate a mentor and ask pertinent questions.

You may always do your research. You must always work to increase your knowledge. Your critical thinking skills will improve as a result of that method of thinking.

Remember that information is all around us. You can find more answers than you can think with Google and Youtube.

5. The question "Am I Right?”

Some young people need to respond better to constructive criticism. They take offense when someone instructs them on how to do or perform something properly.

Someone who has the authority to reprimand them, such as parents, teachers, or mentors. They believe they are under assault. Objectiveness is, in fact, a critical thinking skill that every adolescent must acquire. Being objective will help you think more critically in general. Additionally, it will alter your outlook and way of life.

Young people do not have to concur with everything that is said to them. However, they must be able to determine whether the advice will be helpful to them or not. And that's where the ability to think critically is useful.

Among other things, they require to be analytical and open-minded. Teens who want to start their businesses need to recognize that they will get both good and negative criticism along their entrepreneurial journey.

But always remember that if the recommendation comes from a reliable source, someone who cares and has your best interests in mind, then you should take it into consideration.

Keep sight of how youthful you are. Life will teach you many things in the future, but for now, you are still a child who needs to grow. Always maintain objectivity, and don't attempt to avoid receiving critiques on your work.

Additionally, this implies that you must use your judgment. Making conclusions and taking in other people's criticisms are necessary to develop critical thinking skills.

6. Strengthen Your Strengths and Address Your Weaknesses

Some young people could believe they are inferior to others. They often feel worthless since they need clarification about what to do. But we all have our strengths. A few of them are subconsciously present in our hearts and only need awareness.

Get a paper. List everything you excel at or where you are strong in one column, and list all the areas you need to boost in a separate column.

Knowing your strengths and weaknesses helps you to understand better the course you should pursue. Now list what you'll do to improve yourself in a third column.

Make sure to make improvements. Start right away when you place your pencil on the table. Remember that addressing problems is a critical thinking skill. There is nothing more you can do except solve your problems. Keep in mind that, if done well, these behaviors would have a significant impact on your achievement.

7. Make it Simple

"This can be simpler said than done," some people would remark. Hey, however, it's easier than you think. The process of honing your critical thinking skills may be enjoyable and fascinating.

Teens often feel pressure when they must do a whole new task. The issue also affects adults. Therefore, it is irrelevant how old you are. If your critical thinking abilities stay the same for a while, it's nothing to be concerned about.

It takes time to grow into the best possible version of oneself since this process is lengthy. Don't worry about running out of time. Understand that mastering critical thinking is a lifelong endeavor. So, savor every second of your progress and remember what you learned from the journey.

Taking Responsibility for Your Actions is next in Chapter 9. See you there

CHAPTER 9

TAKING RESPONSIBILITY FOR YOUR ACTIONS

Because of the stress and unpredictability of life, it might be easier to avoid accepting responsibility for our actions. That's because it might be challenging to take responsibility for our actions.

It is natural to forget responsibilities to numb unpleasant feelings temporarily, yet doing so might have serious long-term effects. Accepting responsibility for your actions may be liberating and have enormously good effects on your life, even if it is no simple task.

It may strengthen your capacity to study, improve your relationships, and make you feel more in charge of your life.

One of the finest things you can ever do is to take action and accept responsibility for what is happening in your life. You may create your future when you take responsibility for what is occurring in your life.

Taking responsibility for your deeds is crucial for developing enduring connections, improving yourself, and assisting you in taking charge of your life.

What does it entail to accept responsibility for your actions?

By accepting responsibility for your actions, you stop blaming them on other people or outside forces and take ownership of the benefits and drawbacks of your decisions and conduct.

It might be more challenging to acknowledge the results of certain actions than to place the blame for bad outcomes on external factors or other individuals. In the long term, accepting accountability for your acts shows you have character and are eager to develop. When you accept responsibility for your actions, you become aware of the aspects of your life that you can influence and improve.

It also entails letting go of the things you can't change without blaming or making excuses. It might be challenging to own our mistakes and take concrete actions to fix them.

Our first response can be to assign blame to others or provide justifications for the circumstance.

You have the ability to control your life when you accept responsibility for your deeds, and you may choose how you react to events rather than merely responding to them.

When you accept responsibility for your actions, whether a mistake you made or a situation you would want to alter; you must first identify the problem.

After that, you become aware of your part in the circumstance, including the elements within your control and those you cannot alter.

Finally, you put your action plan into action to fix the problem and lessen the likelihood that it will occur again in the not-too-distant future.

Why is it crucial to accept accountability for your actions?

It may be challenging, but accepting responsibility for your actions offers numerous advantages.

Here are four of the biggest advantages of accepting accountability for your actions:

1. It enhances psychological well-being.

Studies demonstrate that "developing personal responsibility adds to one's happiness, self-esteem, and mental health by enabling people to take ownership of their behaviors and activities."

Instead of feeling like someone who was the victim of circumstance, you get a sense of control when you accept responsibility for your actions. To be responsible for your actions, you must actively participate in problem-solving rather than passively assuming that things will work themselves out.

Environmental circumstances that are beyond our control will have a big impact on mental health and well-being.

There will be some things you can adjust. Say, for instance, that you are battling anxiety and wish to accept responsibility for enhancing your mental health.

You might investigate what coping mechanisms, such as deep breathing, meditation, exercise, looking after a pet, or bonding with loved ones, are effective for you, and you might try to gain a deeper comprehension of your triggers.

Every single one of these things is under your control and is likely to make your symptoms get better over time.

2. It improves your connections.

Consider your intimate connections. Would you want to surround yourself with a person who refuses to accept responsibility for their actions, continually assigns blame to others, and makes excuses for everything they do?

No, is the likely response. Because the person may come out as not trustworthy and unreliable. Relationships depend on you being accountable for your actions.

Doing this shows your friend or relatives that you are responsible and open to being vulnerable. It, in turn, creates a setting where the other person feels comfortable being honest and genuine, which fosters relationships that are defined by confidence, honesty, and transparency.

3. It enhances your capacity for learning.

There has been substantial research on the connection between personal accountability and cognitive performance. According to research, self-directed learning is crucial for success in school, in one's personal life, and in one's career.

When students accept responsibility for their learning, they acknowledge that they actively contribute to it and that their decisions impact their peers.

Strong learning involves doing more than passively absorbing information, which is what it means to be a good learner. Instead, the strong learner assumes responsibility for their learning by investing effort and engagement in their studies and having a stake in them.

4. Your internal locus of control will increase.

According to psychology, a person with an internal locus of control feels in charge of their life rather than feeling as if other forces are in control of it.

You are more inclined to ascribe your likelihood of succeeding and even failing to your activities if you have a greater internal locus of control.

You can think that you have no control over your life and that any success or failure you encounter is the result of destiny or chance if you have a greater external locus of control.

Say, for instance, that a significant test is forthcoming at school. A person with a greater internal locus of control could study more diligently because they think their preparation and study habits will show in their test outcomes.

On the other side, someone with a stronger external locus of control could think studying is pointless since the outcome of the test is beyond their control and dependent on the instructor's bias.

- Who do you believe will do better in this circumstance?

People with an internal locus of control accept accountability for their actions because they are aware of the areas of their lives that they control and act accordingly.

According to studies, those who have a stronger sense of internal control are more resilient to stress and have higher levels of self-assurance.

How to Begin Taking Responsibility for Your Actions

As it stands out, there are several benefits to accepting responsibility for your actions. But how exactly do you do that?

Here are some pointers to assist you in accepting responsibility.

1. Quit placing blame on others.

Blame is protection. Instead of accepting complete responsibility for your actions, it is simpler to blame others for problems or mistakes.

It does not follow that something is correct or advantageous to you in the long run simply because it is simpler. Shifting the blame at the time may help reduce some tension and unpleasant feelings, but it won't solve the problem, and you'll probably feel guilty and emotionally spent.

It is unfair to both you and the one who was incorrectly accused. Furthermore, blaming others risks your relationships, jobs, and other important relationships.

You can feel alone if others stop respecting and trusting you. It might be frightening to accept responsibility and move toward change. You may find it easier to avoid the "blame game" and accept responsibility for your actions if you remind yourself that doing the right thing will ultimately benefit you.

2. Avoid excuses.

We may come up with justifications for why we didn't accept responsibility for our actions or for avoiding challenging or unpleasant circumstances. Making excuses is equivalent to choosing the easy route.

We employ justifications for our behavior, even though they may be incorrect, rather than owning up to our faults or errors.

For instance, it's possible that you were unable to complete a school task in time. Consider the variables within your control before criticizing the instructor for setting the deadline too soon.

You might have begun the work early enough to finish it on time, or you could have asked a peer or an instructor for help so that you could finish the job. Making justifications for our actions might be alluring, but doing so is counterproductive and won't help you in the long run.

3. Perceive unfavorable feelings.

You will inevitably encounter unfavorable feelings throughout your life. Accepting responsibility for your actions might make you feel uneasy, afraid, and ashamed.

Although accepting these feelings is difficult, doing so is necessary if you want to move on. You may learn to sit with uncomfortable feelings rather than attempting to avoid them by engaging in mindfulness exercises.

Avoiding unpleasant feelings and suffering prolongs it over time, making it more challenging to accept responsibility for our actions and achieve progress.

When experiencing negative emotions, try to practice mindfulness.

4. Act instead of reacting.

Our natural tendency is to get defensive when errors or unpleasant circumstances occur.

As was already said, shifting responsibility, providing justifications, or avoiding unpleasant feelings might sometimes be simpler. Without carefully considering our actions, we often respond in a defensive manner that doesn't address the problem.

It's critical to take one step back and respond to the issue composed and effectively. In the heat of the moment, it may be hard to maintain a level head, but there are several things you can do to help yourself calm down so you can move on:

- Exercise
- Practice deep breathing

- Take a brief stroll
- Make a call to a friend to discuss the matter.

You are better equipped to decide how to address the circumstance if you are in a position where you are acting rather than reacting.

5. Put self-care into action.

We all make mistakes, experience tough times, and behave in ways we later regret. No one is flawless, and everyone encounters this. Being nice to oneself is just as crucial as accepting responsibility for our acts and making things right.

Say, for instance, that after getting into a heated dispute with a close friend, you are now beating yourself up over it.

You might be persuading yourself that you are a nasty person who doesn't deserve friendship as you obsess over the discussion, reflecting on the things you said or should have said. Although these unfavorable ideas and emotions are normal and legitimate, they do not improve the circumstance or allow self-compassion.

Imagine a buddy approached you with the same issue. How would you respond to them?

You most likely would act compassionately and say anything like:

"That seems like a challenging scenario, and I can tell you're not satisfied with how you handled it. Keep in mind that mistakes are inevitable, and things will get better.

What do you believe you can do to make things better? By adopting this strategy, you may be compassionate to yourself and forgive yourself while still holding yourself responsible and accepting responsibility for your actions.

In the next Chapter, you will learn How to Cultivate a Positive Attitude. Happy Reading.

CHAPTER 10

CULTIVATE A POSITIVE ATTITUDE

Your teen years are complex, whether figuring out who you are, taking on fresh tasks, or fretting about fitting in. Having a positive attitude while facing problems may be more challenging, but doing so will improve your stress management, health, and the likelihood of overcoming obstacles and achieving your objectives.

Positivity has limitless power. You need to understand that living a terrible life will only negatively affect them. Things are different when it comes to having a good mental attitude.

Do you know what the law of attraction is? That will be the topic we have to discuss. I'll give you an example.

Teen boys often struggle with a lack of confidence. They want to achieve but need a genuine belief in their abilities. A typical teen boy wants to start his own company but is worried about failing.

If failure is all you think about, it will happen. More specifically, you'll draw it to you.

So what is the answer to this issue? You only need to entirely alter your perspective and attitude, which is simple.

Advantages of a Positive Attitude

It might be difficult to have a good outlook when so many issues are going on in the world. An inexperienced teen finds it particularly challenging. Finding something to spur you on to change will be the first thing you need to accomplish.

Benefits and the power of a positive attitude may be a real motivators. So let's discuss it!

1. Productivity

Productivity is the first benefit a positive will provide you.

Imagine you wish to do well in school and graduate with a high grade. However, you can't stop thinking about your daily problems with life.

For instance, financial obligations, doubt, relationship issues, etc.

Will you have the capacity to concentrate on your studies? You'll be surprised at how much you can do in a single day if your mind is manageable with distractions.

2. Confidence

How often have you regretted not taking a certain action in the past? Most of the time, you were afraid of making a mistake. You can be confident that changing your mindset will affect the situation.

At last, you will understand your worth and what you are capable of. As I previously said, having a positive attitude will boost your productivity. That implies that you will begin accomplishing your mini-goals every day. We'll feel more confident once our ideas come to fruition.

Children seldom get the chance to exercise their abilities. The majority of them want to remain in their familiar surroundings because they feel comfortable there.

But positivity is necessary to leave your comfort zone. You can only achieve success "out there" in that manner.

3. Positive Minded People

All of us require a positive environment. Our whole lives can benefit from that kind of atmosphere. However, positive people only want to interact with other positive people. They aim to prevent others from destroying their positivity.

Having a positive attitude will attract such kinds of individuals. You'll associate with positive-minded folks who are genuine believers in achieving achievement.

An optimistic person consistently holds out hope for a favorable outcome, and they think that everything occurs for a good cause, even in bad times.

Being pessimistic from a young age might have detrimental effects. You'll start hanging around with individuals who have no convictions, aspirations, or goals. You will eventually get used to and adjust to that kind of person.

Unfortunately, such young people continue to struggle throughout their lives, and they continue to struggle in every aspect of their lives.

Don't you want to stay away from that? You have a better understanding of the influence of a positive.

4. A helpful influence

Teenagers should also be aware that having a positive attitude in life has a wider impact. Additionally, it has the power to alter the lives of those close to you, and specifically, you'll make a good impression on the people you love.

Their lives may become more lovely and joyful due to our optimism. The most wonderful thing you will have accomplished will be the feeling of pride you will have.

How to Cultivate a Positive Attitude

You may do a few actions to increase your positive attitude.

1. Be objective

You should start by asking yourself, "Am I positive or not? " Many individuals do not like to acknowledge that they need to work on their attitude. They would prefer to take responsibility for their mistakes elsewhere since that should be the simplest action.

It makes sense for you to think highly of yourself as a teen boy. However, you should honestly assess your positive and negative aspects. You are prepared to go on to the next phase after "meeting" yourself.

2. Examine Your Memories

Using your memories, you may better comprehend the full power of a positive attitude. Since it is impossible for there to be just negative experiences in your life, try and recall parts of your life that were fun and interesting. The most lovely aspect of your existence is unquestionably there. That memory can make your day better.

In addition, you may find inspiration in your development process. You were only a little child who knew nothing about life five years ago. You changed into a person who is capable of achieving significant goals in only five years.

In five years, what do you think will happen? You still have time to do and enjoy a lot of nice things.

Create a "To-Do" list.

- What plans do you have for today?
- What are your plans for tomorrow?
- That is okay if you wish to go "offline" once a week.

The idea of life is to use more time to do something significant. Your positive attitude will decline as you begin to feel ineffective.

To-do lists resemble assignments. It is a list of tasks with deadlines that are clear.

You should give yourself homework if you need something important you are doing. For instance, you'll look for your passion today. Tomorrow's job may be to do some study on the industry in which you want to operate in the future.

Each of your responsibilities must be worthwhile to you in some way, and completing it once at a time will increase your optimism and attitude. You'll eventually develop the mentality of "I can do it."

4. Elimination of Distractions

Numerous distractions are always present when maintaining a positive attitude.

These distractions serve as a warning against excessive relaxation, and you should try to find a way to put these distractions to rest. It is hard to develop a positive attitude when you are overwhelmed with distractions.

5. Show gratitude!

Positive thinking is synonymous with being appreciative. Let's take a scenario that most high school students encounter.

- Do any students at your school have wealthy or influential parents?
- What do you think when you see that they can afford everything that you hoped to be able to buy?
- Do you experience any negative emotions or thoughts when you consider these things?

You should refrain from following such a practice. It will keep you from developing a really good mindset and positive attitude. Over time, your thoughts will progressively turn negative.

You have a responsibility to express gratitude for what you have. Most individuals often refrain, "It can't be worse."

The worst is always a possibility, but the best is also! Pay attention to what you already have. Be thankful that you have the chance to succeed in life. Thank your parents for always being there for you by being grateful to them and always practicing gratitude

In general, you may change your mentality and life in this way, and complaining and discontent are inappropriate.

6. Have faith in yourself

We should clarify the distinction between responsible behavior and irresponsible behavior. Some believe that simply telling someone "everything will be okay" will suffice. Indeed, it is preferable to declare, "I'm going to fail."

However, adopting a positive outlook necessitates remaining upbeat as you work to resolve your issues. I don't advise you to sit in your room and wait for things to be ideal.

You must be ready for whatever issues you encounter and have faith in your ability to overcome them.

7. Try new things

We must attempt new things to create whatever changes we want. You will have to attempt things you were frightened of in this situation.

Let's use entrepreneurship as an example. Since there are some risks involved, many teenagers would prefer to find a full-time job in the future. Remaining in your comfort zone is an additional approach to maintaining a bad attitude.

Why?

As a result of your inability to try new things, identify your abilities and potential.

With that type of attitude, you won't comprehend the true worth of who you are. Remember that we are all immensely precious, even if not all of us are aware of it.

With a positive attitude, your mind will grow so powerful, and you won’t be afraid to try new things.

In Chapter 11, I will teach you how to Practice Empathy and Understanding toward Others. See you there.

CHAPTER 11

PRACTICE EMPATHY AND UNDERSTANDING TOWARD OTHERS

The capacity to comprehend and experience another person's experiences and emotions is known as empathy.

Building strong connections is crucial for your professional and personal lives, and empathy is vital in building healthy relationships.

Empathizers are stereotyped as being aloof and self-absorbed, often living lonely lives. Empathy is infamously absent in sociopaths. On the other hand, empathy makes a person seem kind and compassionate.

A strong factor that supports societal harmony and collaboration is empathy, it is an attitude that enables individuals to comprehend and interact with others. It is also the emotion that makes it hard to ignore the pain of others.

There are many advantages to happiness for empathic persons. Empathy often promotes generous conduct, and empathy-based compassion has been shown to boost cooperation and forgiveness, build relationships, and reduce hostility and judgment, in addition to boosting both physical and mental well-being. It also has been found to increase compassion.

To increase happiness for ourselves and others, it is crucial to exercise empathy regardless of how we are feeling. You may improve your comprehension of and interactions with the people in your life by practicing empathy.

How to Develop Empathy

1. Set listening as a top priority.

First, you must identify the emotion someone else is experiencing to empathize with them. While important, listening is only sometimes simple.

The intensity in a close friend's voice generally grabs your attention right away when they call and need to vent about how difficult things have been since their new split or how difficult school has been for them.

It becomes more challenging when interactions are taking place among interruptions and have less overt emotional content. Empathy starts when you decide to listen to emotions.

Please pay attention to the cues others give off that might reveal their emotional states. Since when it comes to being aware of what others are experiencing, your emotions might be a huge obstacle.

You could not be giving the other person enough attention while discussing if you are thinking about your own emotions and how you can express them. You may improve your capacity for empathy and emotional understanding by attempting to listen actively.

2. Express Emotions

Empathy puts you directly in the other person's shoes once you can detect their feeling. Empathy isn't feeling how you might feel in that circumstance; it's standing by someone else and temporarily taking on their emotions.

According to some studies, mirror neurons—brain circuits that light up whether we are experiencing the stimulus ourselves or watching someone else experience it—are the reason we are successful in experiencing their emotion of theirs.

Mirror neurons make you jump up and down in agony when you see horrible mistakes in a humorous viral video or get your pulse pumping as you see athletes race across a stadium at the sport you love event.

This empathy not only enables one to stand by another and comfort them with greater compassion, but it also conveys the message that one is prepared to take on a difficult feeling so that others don't have to go through it alone.

3. Be vulnerable

Your relationships may be improved by allowing yourself to experience another person's emotions completely, and such connections can be strengthened by letting yourself be vulnerable to others.

Sharing difficult emotional experiences, such as guilt, fear, and shame, gives people a chance to relate to you.

Being open to vulnerability improves empathy in two ways. First, seeing the worth of empathy when returned to you helps strengthen your resolve to empathize with others. Additionally, you become more adept at handling difficult emotions in social interactions.

It's difficult to maintain a discussion about unpleasant feelings. Still, if you consciously develop this skill by seizing the chance to express your emotions, you'll be more prepared to be on the receiving end.

4. Act and Offer Assistance

Happiness may diminish if empathy consists of sharing bad feelings. People become more adept at placing themselves in the shoes of others when they experience intense grief for survivors of a natural catastrophe.

However, merely sharing someone else's suffering doesn't fully utilize the chance to improve well-being, even though doing so may increase connection and understanding. Knowing what another individual is experiencing helps you better understand what individuals need.

Since empathy involves embracing the emotion but not the trying circumstances that gave the cause for it, you are typically in a stronger position to assist. Empathy works best and promotes well-being when you can sense another person's suffering while knowing that you can alleviate it.

People with high empathy levels were more likely to intervene and assist even when they had the option to turn away and stop watching in a classic experiment where those who participated watched somebody else get electric shocks and offered the option to assist them by taking the remainder of the shocks themselves.

Participants could feel the shock's anguish just enough to want to assist, but not as much that they were unwilling to take the burden onto themselves. It is known as effective empathy.

5. Make an effort.

Take on difficult tasks requiring you to go outside your comfort zone. Learn a new skill, like how to play a musical instrument, a new hobby, or a foreign language.

Create a new professional skill. You will become more humble if you act this way because humility is a crucial facilitator of empathy.

6. Leave your familiar surroundings.

Particularly to unfamiliar locations and cultures. It improves your understanding of other people.

7. Request input.

Request criticism on your social and interpersonal skills. For instance, ask your family and friends to listen to you, and afterward, check in with them from time to time to see how you're doing.

8. Read books.

Read books that examine intimate relationships and feelings. There is evidence that suggests this helps teenagers' empathy.

9. Take a step in their shoes.

Discuss with others what it feels like to be in their position, their problems and worries, and how they viewed the events you two had.

10. Consider your prejudices.

We all have unconscious prejudices and sometimes overt ones, which limit our capacity for empathy and listening. These frequently revolve around observable characteristics like gender, race, and age.

Do you not believe that you are prejudiced? Reconsider; we all do.

11. Develop a curiosity-driven mindset.

- What exactly can you learn from a youthful, "inexperienced" coworker?

- What exactly can you learn from your "narrow-minded classmate?

Curious people frequently ask questions, which helps them gain a deeper understanding of those around them. Not only can empathy help you comprehend others, but it may also inspire you to take action and change the world.

It becomes more powerful when you use empathy as a driving force to take action—whether that means comforting a buddy, purchasing a little present for someone in need, or contributing to organizations that support victims of natural disasters.

Be careful to listen and share when you notice someone else struggling, but also be sure to say what you can do to assist. Empathy follow-through entails starting good change for other people. The wonderful thing concerning empathy is that it enhances your personal growth, and others start to develop.

Mastering Listening Skills is next in Chapter 12. Happy Reading.

CHAPTER 12

LISTENING SKILLS

Life success depends on strong communication skills; listening is crucial to good communication. Evaluating and improving your listening skills may be helpful in work settings and beyond.

Communication is more crucial than ever in today's high-tech, hot-speed, high-stress world. Nevertheless, we spend less and less time genuinely listening to one another. The gift of time has become rare, and genuine listening has declined.

Listening skills foster communication, resolve issues, ensure comprehension, settle disputes, and increase accuracy. Effective listening in school improves relationships and academic performance.

Effective listening at work results in fewer mistakes and less time spent. At home, it fosters the growth of resourceful, independent kids who can find solutions to their problems.

Our listening skills impact every part of our life. As a teen boy, you need to learn to listen better to enhance your academic, professional, and personal life. You will stand to better your professional, intellectual, social, and emotional lives if you can master the skill of listening.

In this chapter, I'll discuss the value of listening skills, why developing them might be challenging, how to do so, and how to listen more carefully.

Everyone values communication with friends, family, colleagues, or the individuals you meet daily. But it's important to recognize that different people communicate in different ways.

Why is listening to a valuable skill?

Effective communication depends on having practical listening skills. Being a good listener may help you build stronger bonds with other people, make better judgments, and come to swift agreements with others.

Below are the reasons to develop your listening skills:

- It shows your capacity to pay close attention to someone else's opinions, actions, and feelings.
- Increases your capacity to serve, inspire, and develop others successfully.
- Improves social skills.
- Creates interpersonal and professional connections

Developing your Listening Skills.

It might be helpful to assess your present listening skills to identify areas that want development. Here are some suggestions about how to become better at listening:

1. Establish eye contact

Avoid glancing out the window, texting, browsing through your smartphone, or checking a computer screen while someone is talking. Avoid unwanted interruptions, give the speaker your attention, and make eye contact.

It gives them a nonverbal indication that you are paying attention to what they have to say, which motivates them to keep talking. Be aware that the speaker could not be making direct eye contact with you because they are uncomfortable or shy or their culture forbids it. You should keep facing the speaker even if they don't meet your eye contact.

2. Put the speaker's words into your own words.

To assist you in remembering what you hear, try to visualize what the speaker is discussing while you listen. It might be a literal illustration or other ideas connected to the subject.

As you listen for a long time, this will make it easier for you to recall the words and phrases. You won't need to get ready for what to say next if you can remember what the speaker is saying, and if you find yourself drifting off, be sure to get back on track right away.

3. Restrict judgments.

Listen without judging the speaker. Despite the fact that the message makes you anxious or agitated, try to stop thinking about critical or judgmental remarks since doing so impairs your capacity to pay attention.

Listen with an open mind and recognize that the other person is sharing their perspective with you. As they talk to you further, you might notice that they make clearer sense, and you will only fully understand the story if you listen without being cynical.

4. Avoid interruptions

Each person analyzes information and talks at their own pace. If someone is speaking slowly, try to be patient and allow for them to complete before attempting to speed things up by anticipating what they will say next or responding before they have done speaking.

Interrupting conveys that what the speaker is saying doesn't mean much to you. It might imply that what you've got to say is more significant than what they have to say, that you are uninterested in what they say, or that the discourse is competitive.

It's also crucial to avoid interruptions. People primarily want you to listen. Nevertheless, if you have a great idea, consider getting permission to share it before speaking.

5. Await a lull before asking questions.

It's possible that you need to comprehend everything someone says. It is better to wait until they stop before requesting clarification on the subject or word you didn't understand.

6. Request clarification.

Seeking clarification helps steer the discussion in the right direction. Instead of asking a question regarding anything unrelated to the significant point the speaker is attempting to make, you should only ask questions that are relevant to the discussion.

It demonstrates that you are listening, paying attention, and prepared to discuss things further when you offer clarifying questions without interjecting.

7. Feel the speaker's emotion.

For listening to be successful, empathy is necessary. It would be best if you expressed yourself as the speaker does.

Your appearance, expressions, and words should portray the same feelings as theirs if their face expresses grief or delight. It requires effort and focuses on empathizing with the speaker, yet it promotes connections and open communication. Empathy plus emotional intelligence are the cornerstones of effective listening.

If you feel sad when the individual you're speaking to expresses sorrow, delighted when they show happiness, and concerned when they express anxiety, you're listening well.

You may convey this via your words and facial gestures. By putting yourself in the position of the other individual and allowing yourself to experience what it would be like to be in that situation, you may develop empathy. It is hard to do and needs a lot of focus and work. Whatever the case, it will drastically improve the caliber of your interactions.

8. Be aware of nonverbal clues

Nonverbal communication is one kind of interpersonal communication. When someone is speaking with you, their facial expressions and tone of voice may reveal a lot about them—observing someone's eyes, lips, and shoulder posture. In contrast, speaking makes it simple to determine if they are bored, excited, or irritated. As a result, listening also entails observing nonverbal signs.

9. Offer the speaker your thoughts

Both vocal and nonverbal feedback is possible. Using verbal feedback, you can say things like,

"OK," or "I realize that must be challenging." You may communicate nonverbally by shaking your head and making the correct facial expressions. The idea is to tell the speaker you are paying attention by sending cues.

When someone gives you instructions, repeat the job list so they know you understand what to complete. Another sign of attention is writing down what they say.

10. Develop your hearing

Being conscious of your actions when someone is speaking to you can help you improve your listening skills. You can take notes after an in-person conversation or listen to podcasts and audiobooks without the text on the screen.

To test how much knowledge you can remember, try listening to recordings that are no longer than four minutes and playing them again. It may improve your general communication skills and make you more conscious of your function as a recipient of information.

11 Pay attention, but be calm.

When you establish eye contact with the speaker, you're not required to keep your eyes fixated on the other individual. You can sometimes turn your head away and go about your business as usual.

The most crucial thing is to pay attention. Attending someone means being there. Remove distractions from your mind, such as noise and background activities. Additionally, try not to pay too much attention to the speaker's accent or speech patterns to the point in which they turn into a hindrance, and avoid letting your prejudices, beliefs, or emotions get in the way.

12. Remain flexible.

Pay attention without passing judgment on the speaker or critiquing what he says in your head. You may be worried if what he says scares you, but you shouldn't think, "Well, that was a dumb move."

From the moment you start making cynical jokes, you lose the ability to listen well. Pay attention without making judgments. Keep in mind that the speaker is expressing their emotions and ideas through words. Listening is the only means by which you will learn what those feelings and thoughts are.

13. Be careful not to sentence-grab.

Some people sometimes attempt to speed up the pace of conversations by interrupting and completing sentences since they can't slow their mental rate down enough to listen properly. There are better ways to communicate and listen.

Learning Basic Self-defense Skills is next in Chapter 13.

CHAPTER 13

LEARN BASIC SELF-DEFENSE SKILLS

Everybody, including teenage boys, should have the right to defend themselves physically from harm. In today's world, we often ignore the need to teach kids how to defend themselves, despite the fact that doing so is crucial.

It is crucial for teen boys to be capable of self-defense in this day and age when school bullying is a significant issue. Self-defense not only enables teen boys to protect themselves against physical assaults effectively, but it also has other positive effects on their daily lives.

Discipline, resilience, and persistence are essential values and concepts that may be learned.

You might be in danger from bullying or something much worse as a teen boy. Therefore, it is crucial you learn self-defense. Self-defense is a valuable skill that safeguards and even boosts your confidence.

The Importance of Self-defense for Teenage Boys

1. It Arms Teen boys With Self-Defense Knowledge

As previously established, everyone has the right to self-defense, even teens.

Teen boys who learn self-defense may become more independent and, of course, take on more responsibility. Please don't see it as combat. Teens who learn self-defense will learn how and when to use their knowledge and talents.

Self-defense teaches teen boys that they should only use their bodies to protect themselves from any threats, not to hurt other people.

2. It Aids in Combating the School Bullying Epidemic

Every parent's worst nightmare is bullying. We often hear about it taking place in classrooms, parks, and even in the social circles of our children.

We fear the day when we learn that either our kid is bullying someone else or they are bullied by someone else. Bullying in schools is an ongoing issue. Despite society having made significant efforts to eradicate bullying from our educational institutions, bullying still occurs today.

In some ways, the issue is as severe as it has ever been. By learning self-defense skills, teens can put a stop to bullying. Any particular child could be a bully or a target of a bully. Teen boys who learn self-defense might gain self-assurance, self-control, respect for themselves, and respect for others.

Developing these crucial personality qualities may help put an end to bullying once and for all since the change needs to originate from inside ourselves. Learn self-defense skills, and see the instant difference it makes in your life.

3. It Instills in Teen Boys Responsibility and Discipline

Self-defense instills responsibility and discipline in teen boys, and it is crucial for their development since we must all exercise self-control and accept responsibility for our conduct.

Self-defense teaches teen boys that it isn't important whether or not you fall to the ground; the ability to stand back up and continue moving ahead is what counts.

Self-defense Techniques All Teenage Boys Should Know

1. Believe in your instincts

Too many people sign up for self-defense classes after being attacked. When describing the attack, they often state the same about an incident: "I got this uneasy feeling, but I told myself not to be crazy."

"I knew I shouldn't have gone, but I didn't want to upset his emotions," or something like that. The primary line is that it generally is only safe if something feels right.

Many individuals have been trained to disregard the nagging voice that warns them disaster is ahead. It would be best if you understood that your gut feeling is the most excellent danger detector. When you hear that small voice again, please pay attention to what it has to say.

2. Avoid presenting yourself as a target.

Avoid an attack before it happens by not presenting yourself as a target. Please take advantage of whatever chance you have to leave a precarious situation before it becomes worse.

Move to the opposite side of the street if a coming person gives you a bad feeling.

Always look out for dangerous situations and try to avoid them. That behavior is not cowardly; rather, it is a wise strategy for avoiding danger.

3. Demonstrate self-assurance.

The signals your body conveys to people around you should be considered.

Like animals, humans prey on individuals they believe to be most vulnerable or weak. Attackers look for targets who seem scared, weak, or preoccupied.

They search for those who stroll with their heads down and their hands in their pockets, possibly one full of packages or preoccupied with their phone. Keep in mind that attackers want an easy target rather than to provoke a confrontation.

4. Establish very strict verbal boundaries.

Practical self-defense requires good communication skills, which you're more likely to employ regularly and more effectively than any physical method.

When an assailant converses with you, you're being "interviewed" to see whether you'll make a suitable victim. An adept attacker is skilled at employing this tactic. He wanted you to be so terrified by what he said that you wouldn't attempt to defend yourself.

Although engaging in a combative verbal exchange can be frightening, you must have the fortitude to demonstrate that the attacker chose the incorrect victim.

They will leave you alone if you carry yourself with confidence, maintain your composure, and speak assertively.

The strength of your tone alone might make him leave you and search for a weaker victim.

5. Have an element of surprise

One of your hidden tools for self-defense is the element of surprise. Most predators are sure that you won't defend yourself, so to protect yourself, you should take advantage of that misunderstanding.

When you adopt a martial arts posture, the attacker can see right away that you're a skilled fighter. Adopt a self-assured, unhurried posture with your shoulders and hips forward, your arms bent, and your hands raised and out in front of you. He won't be ready for it if you have to strike if that becomes necessary.

6. Keep a Secure Distance

Always strive to keep a possible attacker at least an arm's length away. If you find yourself needing to fight back, you're going to need that distance. Never let a possible danger approach too closely since it takes roughly a quarter of a second to respond to an assault.

Attackers often try to get closer to their targets to determine whether or not they will retaliate. If you lose that test, the attacker will know you are hesitant to fight, which will give them more confidence.

7. Adopt A Non-Aggressive Position

Please take advantage of most victimizers' idea that their victims won't be able to protect themselves by catching them off guard.

When a prospective assailant approaches you, you may do this by adopting a passive posture. Use an open, comfortable posture with your arms out in front of you, shoulders back, and hips forward.

By adopting this posture, you place yourself in a position to protect against or launch assaults rapidly without alerting the possible attacker to your ability to engage in combat or escalate the situation.

8. Maintain simplicity

There are better ideas than using your fancy moves, like spinning heel kicks, in a self-defense scenario. Every time you are in a risky scenario, adrenaline is naturally produced in your body, and one of the repercussions is a loss of fine motor abilities.

Have you ever seen a movie where a victim of axe murder tries to flee and fumbles the door's keys to her haven until the villain finds her?

That's adrenaline at work, and you could have a similar reaction if you need to defend yourself. When adrenaline is coursing through your body, simple tasks like pulling your hands out of your pocket, using a key to unlock a lock, or unlacing your fingers become considerably more difficult.

The worst moment to try sophisticated moves that call for several simultaneous motions is now. If you ever find yourself in a situation where you need to defend yourself, keep it simple.

You should use the following skills for self-defense:

- Heel Palm Strike:

A heel strike has the same force as a closed fist and puts less strain on your hands. Even professional fighters often suffer hand injuries when they engage in combat outside of the ring.

- Eye Strikes:

Self-defense situations are ungoverned; therefore, feel free to use tactics forbidden in competitive sports like mixed martial arts.

MMA fighters often poke their opponents in the eye, and they have up to five minutes to recuperate. Using your lead hand to judge distance and having your fingers extended while doing so will make it simple to poke an attacker's eyes.

- Inside Low Kick

During his reign, Georges St-Pierre possessed one of the finest inside low kicks, which often limited the mobility of his adversaries.

In certain cases, inside low kicks miss their intended target. The inside of the thigh, and instead, fall on the groin. If you can master the inside low kick, you'll have a quick weapon to strike an adversary in the groin.

- Rear Naked Choke:

This one is one of the most straightforward and most efficient chokes utilized in BJJ and other combat sports. No matter how large or powerful the attacker is, a rear-naked choke will stop them.

9. Give emphasis on physical fitness

Being physically healthy increases your chances of effectively defending oneself, particularly if you have experience in martial arts.

Being physically active also lowers your chance of being chosen by predators, who usually choose victims who seem helpless and unable to protect themselves.

Being physically fit reduces the likelihood that prospective attackers would choose you since it suggests that you may be able to turn the tables on them.

Your strength and stamina are the deciding factor if things wind up becoming physical.

10. Employ common sense

When it comes to protecting oneself, common sense is your best tool. By assessing your surroundings and making wise judgments, you may avoid many self-defense scenarios.

Avoid letting your ego push you into increasing conflicts rather than trying to resolve them. For instance, if you run into someone at a party, they could attempt to provoke you into a fight.

You may confront the individual at that time or use verbal judo to defuse the situation. By defusing the situation, you may leave without getting into a fight.

If you don't respond to insults directed at you, some onlookers may think you're a coward or a jerk, but that's their issue, not yours.

Since there are numerous factors beyond your control in any self-defense scenario, the best course of action is to neutralize any possible dangers as soon as they arise.

11. If you are down, don't freak out

When abused, individuals often end up on the ground. The bright side is that most attackers lack proficiency in ground combat; instead, they are bullies who are used to pushing down people and compelling them to submit.

Keep in mind that the heel-palm and eye strikes are effective on the ground. Having a couple of kicks that function there is an excellent idea as well.

The side thrust kick, in particular, is effective in many different circumstances.

If you're on the ground while your attacker is standing, that provides you the edge because then his arms are stretched out. That implies that if he wants to get to you, he will have to reveal his body to your kick.

On the ground, knee strikes are equally useful. Your assailant will likely see you battle with him while he will not shield his groin. Get sufficiently near to strike up into his groin once you spot an opening.

12. Follow through

Until the danger is no longer present, the battle is not ended. As a result, you need to give the fight your all. You forfeit the first benefit from exploiting your initial advantage if you strike back and then halt.

Ensure you utilize the elements of surprise. Because when your adversary realizes you can fight, it is harder for you to win. If you must survive, you must keep hitting until it is safe to stop hitting and get away.

13. Be cautious

If your face is buried in your phone or you're preoccupied with unimportant thoughts, you won't be aware of possible dangers to your safety. Make it a practice to be aware of your surroundings, particularly in areas that you are not familiar with.

Anywhere that is open to the public, such as a roadway or parking lot, is a transitional place. In these areas, predators often choose to attack in the hopes that you won't be paying attention to your surroundings.

The more attentive you are, the easier it will be for you to put the self-defense advice above into practice.

How to Set Realistic and Achievable Goals is next in Chapter 14. Happy Reading.

CHAPTER 14

REALISTIC AND ACHIEVABLE GOALS

To succeed, it's crucial to set realistic and achievable goals. Although setting goals is one step in a process that may help you achieve success, doing so alone does not ensure success.

Setting achievable goals is essential for making plans, carrying them out, maintaining motivation, and, finally, assessing your accomplishment.

Let's first explore the characteristics that make a goal realistic before delving into the significance of creating a realistic and achievable goal.

What does "realistic goal" mean?

To determine what a realistic goal is, there is no precise formula. Depending on a person's abilities, motivation, and desire, they may define what is realistic or unrealistic differently.

However, there is general agreement that goals should be attainable because if you think something is doable, you've already started down the path to success.

A realistic goal is one that you can accomplish, given your abilities, time constraints, and degree of desire. A goal is realistic if you can achieve it, given your existing attitude, degree of desire, time frame, skills, and talents.

Setting realistic goals helps in determining both what you desire and what you are capable of achieving.

The Importance of Realistic and Achievable Goals

Achieving a goal that is too far out of our grasp can lead us to lose motivation; thus, setting a realistic goal is crucial. It's easy to establish too ambitious goals in an effort to impress our parents and friends or to redeem ourselves after a slump in productivity.

It would be best if you comprehended the significance of setting realistic and achievable goals in order to prevent making these errors.

1. Setting realistic and achievable goals boosts self-esteem and confidence.

Setting realistic and achievable goals offers us a feeling of direction. When we understand where we're headed and how to get there, achieving our goals becomes easier.

Realistic objectives go one step further: when you meet the milestones you create for yourself, your self-confidence grows.

Science explains that our bodies produce dopamine during these triumphant times, and this pleasant hormone enhances mood and attention.

Realistic objectives help you stay motivated, and setting clear, achievable goals can help you stay focused. You'll be more inspired to keep moving forward as you get closer to your goal, and the more determined you will be to finish it.

3. Making decisions becomes simpler.

As humans, we make a lot of decisions every day. Whether you're a team leader, a student, or a worker, you sometimes have to make difficult decisions. Having achievable and realistic goals helps the decision-making process move more smoothly when you need to make decisions fast.

4. Achieving realistic and achievable goals takes less time.

It takes a lot of time to accomplish your goals when you need to establish impossible ones. Let's face it, you will only accomplish those ambitious goals and will most likely become weary.

This is why realistic goals need a due date. Wanting to see a 40% improvement in your grade is insufficient. How soon do you want that to happen?

- Thirty days?
- A year?

After you've established the deadline, let everyone know what the time frames and goals are, and this will make cooperation easier.

You may choose to utilize time-tracking software if you need help controlling your time and believe this may be interfering with your capacity to accomplish your set goals.

You'll be able to track how much time you devote to each activity and utilize that data to organize your time more effectively.

5. You become aware of fresh possibilities.

A lack of realistic and achievable goals is like becoming lost in the midst of a jungle without a map. If you don't have a goal to get there, it's simple to feel lost.

Realistic goals provide you with the focus and determination you previously believed you lacked in your life. Setting realistic and achievable goals opens your eyes to a wide range of possibilities.

6. Having realistic and achievable goals will alter your life.

Having goals and a number of checkpoints along the road aids in maintaining our motivation and attention. And ultimately, it's this that has a profound impact on our lives.

When setting goals, beware of these three common errors.

First, to keep your life on track, avoid these three typical goal-setting errors to create realistic and achievable goals and improve your chances of success:

1. Your goal lacks value and depth

Too many times, people only use their thinking to set their goals. If your goals are in line with your values, you have a considerably better chance of success. Examine how your goals and your values—the guiding principles of life you think are significant—align all throughout the goal-setting process by bringing your heart into it.

2. Your goal needs to be more specific.

Your goals should not be vague and ambiguous. Your goals should be SMART (Specific, Measurable, Attainable, Realistic, and Time-Limited) in order to be more achievable.

You may plan how to divide your bigger goals into smaller, more detailed action plans that will advance you after you've created your SMART goals.

3. Your goal needs to have adequate backing.

If you have a coach, cheerleader, or mentor, your chances of achieving your goals will increase. When you work towards your goals, enlist the help and accountability of friends and family. Check-in on your progress and refocus your efforts by returning to your goals often.

How to Set Realistic and Achievable Goals

1. Outline the goals you have.

The first step in achieving a goal is the straightforward act of writing it down. Once you put your goals in writing, they may require more clarification. Reorganize and start again if your documented goals line up differently from the ones you had in mind.

2. Make a resource inventory.

Having the necessary resources and overcoming difficulties is essential for achieving your goals. Make a list of the resources you have at your disposal that may assist you in achieving your goals, as well as any potential obstacles.

These consist of the following:

Time:

Analyze the amount of time you have left to accomplish your goals and if the time frame is within your control. Compile a list of all the activities that can compete for your attention while you are pursuing your goals.

Motivation:

Determine your level of dedication to attaining your goal. Think about if your other obligations could prevent you from achieving your goal.

Information:

Ensure you have the knowledge necessary to accomplish your goals, and to assist you in reaching your goals, do any necessary research.

Training:

Make a list of the abilities you have to accomplish your goals. Continue your training to assist you in achieving those goals.

Funding:

Determine if you have the financial resources necessary to accomplish your goals, and check to see if anything is eating up the funds you need to achieve your goals.

Support:

Find out whether you need any help to achieve your goals. If so, enlist the aid of someone who can assist you in achieving them.

3. Reexamine and make the required adjustments.

You may reevaluate your goals and change them if required now that you've invested the time to write them down and consider the elements that will assist and hinder you in achieving your goals.

You could change your goal to read, "I will put aside thirty percent of my pay for six months as I look for financiers to help launch my new company" If your original goal was "I will set up a new company to provide innovative services to animal-related retail stores," but you lacked the funding to get your business off the ground.

4. Select benchmark

Goal-achieving is a process. Therefore you need checkpoints along the road to see whether or not you're on track, and you may need to adjust your timetable if you miss a milestone.

Additionally, milestones assist you in breaking down everything you have to do into more manageable chunks and helping you see your goals in more detail.

Following a step-by-step process is considerably simpler than attempting to do everything at once.

For example: create reminders for yourself to monitor your achievement every three weeks if you expect it to take six months to complete your goal.

At one of these monitoring times, if you discover that you are running behind schedule, decide if you need to change the timeline or the steps you have planned to achieve your goal.

5. Discuss your goals.

When you share the goals you have with another person, you are inviting accountability for the steps you take to reach them. Friends and family are excellent resources for discussing your goals.

When they inquire about how things are doing, be sure to respond that you value their assistance in keeping you focused. They are assisting you in staying on course to achieve your goals.

6. Take a SMART approach into account.

Use the SMART technique if you want a more organized framework for creating realistic and achievable goals.

How feasible your objectives are is strongly tied to the letters A and R in the SMART acronym. The SMART approach satisfies the following criteria:

- Specific
- Measurable
- Attainable

- Relevant
- Time-based

You will learn how to develop a Strong Work Ethics in the next chapter. See you there

CHAPTER 15

DEVELOP A STRONG WORK ETHICS

The good thing about having a strong work ethic is that it is something that can be learned.

Positive attitude may boost your academic performance and help you establish a solid professional reputation in the future. Before we discuss how to strengthen your work ethic, let's define what work ethic really implies.

What is a "work ethic"?

The capacity to fulfill job obligations with high ethical standards and preserve appropriate workplace values is known as work ethic.

It is a "soft" skill that comes from a person's innate attitude and enables them to carry out their obligations with good moral values, including discipline, collaboration, responsibility, and honesty.

A person with a good work ethic will always examine how their actions will affect others and will draw clear lines between what is acceptable and what is not. Now that we are aware of what work ethics are let's examine what strong and poor work ethics are.

Strong and poor work ethics.

People with strong work ethics develop beneficial habits that make them stand out in every situation. They have learned to develop positive habits like concentrating, maintaining motivation, and completing work without delay. These traits contribute to the development of a strong work ethic and increase output.

Poor work ethics, on the other hand, result in a loss of productivity. Rushing through tasks or waiting until the last minute to finish them sometimes miss deadlines or generates work of inferior quality.

How to Establish a Strong Work Ethics

1. Develop self-discipline.

Be persistent and complete work as promised, and strive for academic excellence in all of your assignments. Anything valuable needs discipline, which entails maintaining attention to long-term objectives while avoiding getting distracted by instant gratification.

Being considerate of others, being truthful and consistent in both your words and deeds, cultivating a reputation for integrity, and practicing being upbeat and courteous helps you to develop self-discipline.

2. Be on time, manage your time well, and maintain equilibrium.

Always arrive early or on time for appointments. You can able to examine your notes or speak with your lecturer if you arrive early for class and keep to your study routine if you are taking classes online.

Focus on finishing all tasks on time since time management is vital for developing a strong work ethic. Don't put off tasks that you can do today; instead, put an end to procrastination.

Knowing how to look after yourself is part of having a strong work ethic. So, eat healthfully, get enough sleep, and take some downtime to unwind. You'll retain the right attitude at school and work if you get your priorities straight.

3. Develop a habit of doing things correctly and a "can do" mentality.

Do things right to achieve the success you desire. Low-quality work results from rushing through tasks, doing shoddy work, not spending enough time preparing, and avoiding doing something altogether if you can't do it well.

By developing a "can do" mentality, you may alter your attitude about your work. A good work ethic entails holding oneself to a high level of performance, which calls for giving your task your all.

4. Establish a reputation for dependability and accountability.

You'll become indispensable at work if you are trustworthy and dependable. Go above the call of duty and offer to help out when needed. Always be on time for deadlines, and be sure to do a good job on any extra tasks you take on.

Create a reputation for always following through on your commitments. Strong work ethics are shown through a great feeling of duty. Be accountable for your actions, take responsibility for mistakes, and take aggressive steps to fix the issues.

It is a personal decision and your individual path; no one can or will assume responsibility for you.

5. Drive and Perseverance.

Strong work ethics place equal emphasis on focus and tenacity. You may teach yourself to work harder and for longer periods of time if you are persistent.

To avoid the danger of burnout, it's crucial to strike a balance between perseverance and enough rest. On the other side, focusing will enable you to complete activities more quickly while preventing distractions.

6. Start each day off on a really positive note and work out often.

How you start your morning will ultimately set the tone for the remainder of your day.

Having a focused and proactive morning routine will aid in the development of a solid work ethic, and establishing a good morning routine can help you build confidence in your abilities to work.

Exercise, music, and meditation are a few examples of morning rituals. When attempting to develop a strong work ethic, be careful not to become a workaholic.

Get some exercise, eat well, and sleep enough. Maintain the proper priorities, and at the end of the day, evaluate your overall life balance. Regular exercise stimulates the mind in addition to being healthy for the body.

Find some challenging exercises that make you work hard. It can assist you in steadily improving and forming a methodical attitude that you may use to forge solid work ethics.

7. Do your best to avoid distractions, and don't let errors stop you in your tracks.

The teen world is rife with distractions. You have access to the Internet via a variety of devices, and it is sometimes difficult to tear yourself away from them. Reading your emails or using social media may eat up a lot of your day's important time and keep you from focusing on what really matters.

Additionally, it will weaken your dedication to your work and have a negative effect on your work ethic. Turn off alerts, check your emails twice or three times each day, and save social media for your downtime at home.

We all make mistakes, on a regular basis. The key is to correct your mistakes quickly, absorb the lessons you've learned, and move on. You can achieve amazing things if you accept failure. Nobody has ever become great without making mistakes along the way.

8. Get Your Day Started Off Right

Whether or not "morning" starts in the late afternoon, evening, or when you'd expect it to, not everybody is a morning person. That problem is not insurmountable, and it's something you should move past.

The initial tasks you do, when you wake up determine your mood and pace for the remainder of the day, and it's crucial to understand your energy cycle.

A significant quality of an excellent work ethic is deliberate production, which may result from the knowledge of your energy circle.

Depending on the time of day, you may do better on certain jobs, such as those that call for more concentration or inventiveness. Self-analysis might be helpful: be aware of your day's energy highs and lows.

It is wise to start your day off with the most vital chores; on the other hand, if you're not a morning person, it may not be the best option.

You might attempt the following to develop healthy and strong work ethics:

- Exercising

- Meditating
- Journaling
- Visual planning

Good exercise produces endorphins, which improve mood and concentration—likewise, meditation.

Learn how to Stay Physically Active as a Teen Boy in Chapter 16. Happy Reading.

CHAPTER 16

STAY PHYSICALLY ACTIVE

As they get closer to reaching their physical maturity, teenagers gain weight and height quickly. They enjoy playing both competitive and non-competitive games, but they would rather spend a shorter period with their parents.

Teen boys feel more independent and important by joining local groups and teams, which gives them a feeling of community and purpose. Due to their seemingly busy schedules and active social lives, they may need help to include physical exercise at this time.

Teen boys should prioritize exercise in their daily life to stay fit and healthy since physical fitness has a range of effects on adolescent health, and lack of physical activity may have negative effects. They should engage in physical activity since it has long-term benefits.

It helps maintain an appropriate physique, which will help to avoid future ailments and increase self-esteem. Teen boys who spend a lot of time engaging in regular physical activity develop a sense of comfort with their bodies.

As a result of their growing confidence in all facets of their lives, they are able to establish a growing number of friends—and it is well-known that friendships made in childhood often last a lifetime.

The advantages of exercise for teenagers

You can maintain excellent health and enhance your general quality of life by being aware of the advantages of physical fitness and understanding the appropriate level of activity.

Here are a few advantages of regular exercise that show how vital physical fitness is.

As an active student, you must juggle the expectations of your family, teachers, coaches, and friends. This could leave you with very little opportunity to concentrate on your own well-being, but if you believe you need more energy or time to work out, think again!

Teen boys may benefit physically and emotionally from physical exercise, which can help them form positive habits and succeed in a range of endeavors.

Even if you've never previously worked out before, you'll most likely become convinced of their benefits after a few trips to the gym.

1. Reduced stress and anxiety

Numerous benefits of regular exercise include a decrease in stress and anxiety. Go for a 30-minute walk or a quick exercise at the gym if you're feeling stressed out due to a friend conflict, a tight deadline, or a family dispute.

You'd be surprised at how much exercise, even for as little as 10 minutes, may help you relax and release stress.

2. Better Skin.

You may keep your youthful glow even after you've finished high school by staying active regularly. In fact, regular exercise from now on will postpone the start of signs of aging. Combine exercise and a healthy diet to reduce acne and look good in your yearbook photo.

3. Less cynicism

Your likelihood of having a good attitude will certainly rise if you approach your exercise with a positive outlook. You may feel good, unwind, and concentrate on your health while working out, which can assist you in tackling any situation with more zeal and confidence.

- Do you worry that you might not pass your midterm?
- Do you get stressed by the daily activity of schoolwork?

Exercise at the gym while listening to your favorite music to see how your perspective shifts.

4. Increased Vitality.

Contrary to popular belief, a demanding workout only sometimes leaves you depleted for the rest of the day. You might experience a substantial gain in energy after exercising.

Whenever you feel fatigued, try going for a quick walk, doing some stretching, or working out.

5. Academic Prowess.

Imagine getting better scores on your next school report sheet as a consequence of your treadmill steps. Exercise is often associated with enhanced academic accomplishment. Increase your concentration in class, your self-confidence, and your brain health by engaging in regular exercise.

6. Improved Confidence

If you want to look fantastic for prom or get into fitness for the upcoming sports season, exercise may help you reach your goals.

Your physical goals could be more easily attained with a sound fitness program, and your emotional, intellectual, and personal goals might be easier to reach thanks to the psychological advantages of exercise.

7. New Companions

Getting in shape is a great way to connect with new people. Begin looking forward to exercising out as a physical or social activity by locating your perfect training companion.

Having a workout partner may increase your enjoyment of the exercise, help you remain accountable, and challenge your limits.

8. A cool positive self-image.

Regular exercise can boost your self-esteem and confidence, giving you the self-assurance you need to nail your next class presentations or ask your crush out on a date.

To develop a higher degree of confidence, challenge yourself in the gym and try different exercises.

9. The ability to lead a healthier lifestyle

Make the most of your life because you only have one. You may succeed in the future through exercising, which has several physical and psychological advantages.

You'll be in a more advantageous position to make choices about your future schooling, work, and interpersonal interactions if you establish healthy habits now while you're still young. There is no better time to start exercising than when you are a teenager, even if you have never done any physical activity.

How to Exercise Physically

Physical activity encompasses much more than simply exercise and relates to your body's capacity to function effectively. Living an active life and taking care of your mental health are both tied to being physically active.

1. Exercise aerobically.

The respiratory and circulatory systems remain healthy with aerobic activity, and your respiratory and circulatory systems eliminate waste from your body and distribute nutrients and oxygen throughout it.

The act of walking, running, and even swimming are examples of cardiovascular exercises that increase heart rate and keep these systems healthy.

Spend 20 to 30 minutes every day engaging in this kind of workout. Combine this exercise with your usual physical activity.

For instance, you should schedule time for a 20-minute walk or another type of exercise, even if you spend a few hours gardening. The greatest method to keep up this habit is to engage in enjoyable activities.

Join a local soccer league if you like the sport, and train on the days you don't have a match.

The best all-around exercise is swimming. If you have sore or tight joints, this low-impact exercise is ideal for you.

2. Make your core stronger.

As you age, having a strong core helps avoid back discomfort and balance problems.

To strengthen the muscles in your stomach, include core workouts into your exercise regimen at least two or three days each week. Basic workouts like crunches and planks are an option, but you can also attempt yoga.

Another choice is Tai chi. Along with strengthening your core, this Chinese martial art also helps with balance and concentration.

3. Lift weight for endurance

Muscles that are in good shape may contract repeatedly for a longer time. Building your muscle endurance involves doing additional sets with lesser weights. Begin with a weight that, after 10–12 repetitions, causes your muscles to feel fatigued.

You can do weightlifting exercises successfully if you learn and apply the appropriate form, and this guarantees you get the maximum benefit and lowers the possibility of harm. By gradually increasing the weight, you may exercise your muscles.

4. Increase strength by lifting big objects.

For improved strength, focus on various muscle groups throughout each workout.

Lighter weights promote muscular endurance, while bigger weights need fewer repetitions to strengthen your muscles. Please start with the lightest weight possible and progressively increase it until your muscles are exhausted after 2 to 5 repetitions.

Plan your strength training workouts in accordance with the amount of time your muscles require to recuperate after a challenging workout—at least 48 hours. Two or three weekly workouts are usually sufficient to maintain your physical fitness.

5. Flexibility-boosting stretches.

Maintain your entire range of motion with stretches, and your fundamental level of physical fitness depends greatly on your flexibility, particularly as you become older.

Stretching is important both before and after exercise since aerobic and other exercises naturally lead your muscles to tighten and stiffen.

A simple yoga practice might be a terrific way to keep your flexibility up. Once you master a few poses, you can also use them as post-workout warm-ups or cool-down stretches. Stretching requires deep, uninterrupted breathing. Stop if you experience any discomfort or stress. It should never hurt to stretch.

6. Consume nourishing meals.

Your health and cognitive performance are both enhanced by proper eating. The optimal diet consists mostly of whole grains, lean proteins, fresh vegetables and fruits, and healthy fats.

Eating healthy meals helps with muscle growth, developing strong bones, fighting off illness, and overall well-being. Establish a routine of serving yourself a healthy quantity and refraining from eating junk and unhealthy foods.

Consume fast food and sweetened beverages and meals in moderation. While having these occasionally is acceptable, including them regularly in your diet will not improve your fitness.

7. Refrain from using drugs and alcohol.

Your mental and physical well-being may be in jeopardy if you use alcohol or drugs. Alcohol use leads to poor physical health and may lead to cardiac issues. Misuse or abuse of other medications may also result in anxiety and depression as well as major health issues.

Ensure that you only consume healthy beverages when you drink, and stop smoking if you do. Your physical fitness will increase, and your chances of coronary artery disease, cancer, and lung disease will decrease if you stop smoking. It may also lengthen your life expectancy by years.

8. Keep hydrated by drinking water.

Your greatest chance of keeping your body hydrated is plain water. Water is necessary for the healthy operation of every aspect of your body.

Let plain water be your go-to beverage, even if you do obtain some water from the meals you consume and other liquids. It works well in your body. Depending on your size and degree of exercise, you need a certain quantity of water to keep hydrated.

You can tell how hydrated you are by looking at the color of your urine; if it's dark yellow or amber, you need to drink more water. To help your body replace the water it loses via perspiration, hydrate yourself before, during, and after an exercise.

Have a bottle of water on hand at all times by carrying one with you. Little sips of water all through the day will keep your body hydrated.

9. Continue to be active all day.

Throughout the course of the day, endeavor to be active for at least an hour total. Sedentary behavior has a negative impact on your health. Despite the fact that you often exercise, if you spend the majority of your time sitting, you cannot reap the full benefits of exercise.

Fortunately, including movement throughout your day is relatively easy.

Here are a few ways:

- Instead of using the elevator, use the steps.
- Work in the garden, on the lawn, or raking leaves in the backyard.
- Organize your house
- Wash the family car
- Take a leisure walk around your neighborhood

10. Sleep for 8-9 hours each night.

A restful night's sleep aids in energy restoration and damage repair. Your physical health will greatly benefit from a regular sleep schedule. Turn off your phone, read a book, or listen to calming music to wind down a little over an hour before you want to go to bed.

Try to maintain a consistent sleep/wake schedule by going to bed and rising at around the same time each day. Keep your sleeping area calm and dark. It is more difficult to go to sleep and into a deep slumber while the light or the TV is on.

Get up and engage in a different thing for a couple of minutes if you're having trouble falling asleep. It won't help to spin about in bed tossing and turning. If you consistently have trouble falling asleep, talk to your doctor. They could suggest a sleep aid as a solution.

11. Enjoy time with loved ones and friends.

The maintenance of your mental health is aided by strong social interactions. Though frequently disregarded, it plays a significant role in physical fitness.

Being in meaningful relationships prevents you from feeling lonely, which might increase your chance of developing depression and other health issues.

You may easily kill two birds with the same stone if you can exercise or engage in additional physical endeavors with family and friends. Their encouragement will greatly inspire you. Another crucial aspect of mental health is hobbies. Sharing your interests with others fosters comradely and friendship.

12. Schedule routine medical exams.

A minimum of once a year, see your doctor. Regular checks aid in the prevention of health issues since your doctor can see early warning signals. You could need more frequent visits to your doctor if you have a persistent medical condition.

Regular visits to your doctor help you build a connection with them. You'll feel more at ease asking them anything if you are used to seeing them.

Summary

Try to engage in 150 minutes a week of aerobic exercise, such as running, to become fit.

To add muscle, perform strength-training routines like minor weightlifting exercises a minimum of twice per week. Eat a minimum of 5 ounces of protein daily, concentrating on lean proteins such as fish, beans, and nuts, to enhance your nutrition.

Make sure you consume 8 glasses of water, 2 cups of vegetables, and 1.5 cups of fruit per day.

Learn how to cultivate a Sense of Gratitude and Appreciation in the final chapter. Thanks for Reading.

CHAPTER 17

CULTIVATE A SENSE OF GRATITUDE AND APPRECIATION

Gratitude has the ability to transform lives. It has the power to lift us out of despair and into a world of hope and brightness. As a result, when it comes to teenage mental health, gratitude, and appreciation may be crucial.

According to studies, practicing gratitude every day promotes self-esteem, empathy, and psychological wellness.

The Impact of Gratitude and Appreciation

Some teenagers don't always naturally express gratitude. We've all heard the cliche of the entitled teen. Part of the reason for this is that young people lack the life experiences or perspective that fosters gratitude. Additionally, it's because they lack the resources necessary to develop the power of gratitude.

Having an "attitude of gratitude" benefits your health and helps you feel better about the everyday challenges and disappointments we all experience.

The Importance of Gratitude and Appreciation

1. Improved sleep.

Gratitude fosters a positive attitude and relaxed mind. Spend a few minutes listing your blessings before going to bed to get a better night's sleep.

2. Improved physical condition.

Some of the physical advantages include reduced blood pressure, boosted immune system, and decreased tiredness.

3. Improved mental state.

Gratitude helps people feel happier and may lessen sadness. It improves resilience as well.

4. More willpower.

Gratitude gives you the willpower to set and achieve your goals. If you want to curb overeating, for example, before a meal, consider the things for which you are thankful to help you resist the need to overeat.

5. A higher sense of self.

Positivity about oneself and one's talents may be attained by cultivating a gratitude mentality and concentrating on all the wonderful things in one's life.

6. Better relationships.

Your relationship with your family and friends might improve when you express gratitude and appreciation. Additionally, it can assist you in creating new, wholesome relationships and friendships.

7. Better self-care.

Being conscious of the positive aspects of your life may encourage actions like regular exercise, a healthy diet, planning time for "me time," and self-care. Gratitude is wonderful because it is cost-free. Additionally, it takes little time to learn and practice.

Aside from that, the advantages are incredible. Making an effort to cultivate appreciation every day has benefits for everyone. You may start feeling more thankful and grateful for the positive things in your life by following the steps below:

1. Keep an eye out for and be appreciative of positive things.

Enjoy, and pay close attention to the pleasant things in your life. Thank someone or express thanks to yourself in writing.

Consider the positive aspects of your life. Start to become aware of and list the things you have to be thankful for. Pay attention to the little, mundane parts of your life and take note of the positives you may sometimes take for granted.

Try the following suggestions:

Write down three things each day for which you are thankful.

- People

- Community.
- Shelter.

Like a warm bed or a satisfying meal, gratitude provides comfort, and it's remarkable what you notice when you give gratitude.

2. Create a notebook of appreciation.

It is more probable that we will notice nice things as they happen if we make a commitment to jot down pleasant things every day.

3. Practice rituals of gratitude.

Before a meal, some individuals say grace. It's a little practice that enables us to recognize and appreciate the gift of having food on the table. It is important to relish the benefits of daily life after you've become aware of them.

4. Enjoy the Gratitude You Feel

There are times when you feel very grateful. You think to yourself, "Oh, wow, this is awesome!" or "How wonderful is this" during these times. Pause. Take note of and savor that real emotion of thankfulness. Soak it all in, and enjoy your benefits as they come to you.

5. Affirm your gratitude

More than politeness, etiquette, or manners, gratitude is a powerful emotion. It's about expressing your sincere appreciation. When you express your gratitude to someone, you are also exercising the first two aspects of gratitude: seeing something positive and showing genuine appreciation for it.

Do this:

- Express your gratitude to someone for a kind deed. Say, "It was very kind of you to..."
- When you..., it greatly assisted me out.
- "When...," you did me a great favor.
- I appreciate you listening when..."
- "I truly valued the lessons you gave me."
- "I appreciate you being there when...."

You may express your thanks in a letter as well.

6. By showing compassion, you may express gratitude.

Your feelings of gratitude may motivate you to do something kind or helpful for someone else. Or you might recognize an opportunity to "pay it forward." Despite the fact that it requires you to wait a little longer than usual, hold the door open for the individual who is coming after you

Perform their chores without letting them know you did them, and take note of how you feel after.

7. Tell the individuals in your life what they mean to you and how you feel about them.

You don't have to be sentimental or extravagant. Each of us has a distinct style. But even a straightforward "Mom, good a delicious meal. Thanks!" can mean a lot if you say it in the right voice and at the right time.

Since you don't want the individual you did a favor for to feel as though you expect something in return, genuine gratitude doesn't make you feel as though you owe them anything. Feeling happy and starting a good cycle are the most important things.

8. Every day, take the time to appreciate nature.

There are many marvels in nature that may astound you and motivate gratitude.

Every day, set aside some time to enjoy the beauty of nature, whether it's a flower, a sunrise, or a bird singing.

9. Good friends don't come around every day, so cherish the ones you already have

Good relationships and connections enrich our lives and provide us with support. Spend time with your friends, talk to them, and show them that you care. Maintaining your friendships will enable you to see the benefits they bring to your life.

10. Be more cheerful.

It's simple to practice appreciation and positivity by smiling. It may improve your mood and the moods of others around you. Try to smile more often, even when you don't feel like it, and see how your disposition and interactions with people change.

11. Make it a practice to do one act of generosity each day.

No matter how little, acts of kindness may have a big influence on both other people and yourself. Whether it's holding the door, praising somebody, or offering to assist, make it a daily aim to do something kind for someone else.

12. Express your affection for your parents.

Your parents are an abundance of love and support for you, yet we're all capable of sometimes taking our parents for granted. Make an effort to show them how much you love them and appreciate all they have done for you.

13. Donate your time to charitable causes.

It's a great opportunity to share and express gratitude for what you have, and it enables you to see things objectively and count your blessings. By enhancing your feeling of purpose and satisfaction, helping others is advantageous to both you and the others you assist.

14. Never slander or defame somebody.

Relationships may suffer when people gossip and talk poorly about others. Look for the positive in individuals and concentrate on the positive things you can say about them.

14. Spend time with the people you love.

Expressing appreciation and fostering relationships require spending time with those we love. Make an effort to push distractions aside and concentrate on the moment at hand while spending time with your loved ones.

15. When your friends and family look good, give them compliments.

A simple method to express your gratitude and increase your friends' and family members' self-confidence is to remember to compliment them when they look good.

It demonstrates your interest in them and appreciation for their efforts.

16. Every day, add at least one new thing to your list of blessings.

By updating your gratitude list a minimum of once every day, you may develop a habit of appreciation and educate your mind to concentrate on the good things in your life.

17. Consider the positive.

When faced with a challenging scenario, it is simple to concentrate on the drawbacks. However, you can change your perspective and find reasons to be thankful by making an effort to see the positives, no matter how insignificant they may seem. It may lead to a happier attitude in life.

18. Make a weekly vow to refrain from grumbling about anything.

It's simple to complain, yet doing so generates a bad vibe that influences not just you but also the people around you. You will be forced to look for solutions rather than focus on issues if you make a commitment not to complain for a week, and you will also start to appreciate the positive aspects of your life.

19. Make an effort to observe when others do well and to acknowledge them when they earn it.

It's important to thank people for their effort and accomplishments. It not only raises spirits but also promotes a pleasant workplace culture. By praising their achievements, you may create a grateful and appreciative culture.

20. Reward effort; repay the favor if somebody does something good for you.

It's vital to let someone know you appreciate what they've done for you. One method to do this is to reciprocate their generosity with a deed of your own. It may spark a domino effect of appreciation and goodwill that is advantageous to everybody.

21. Give thanks for all of your blessings while you meditate while reading your list of gratitude.

A good technique to develop gratitude is meditation. By concentrating on your gratitude list during your meditation practice, you get a greater understanding of the positive aspects of your life, and this leads to a happier outlook and a stronger feeling of well-being.

22. Live in the moment and let go of the past and the future.

Gratitude could be elusive if you're always focused on the past or the future. You may completely enjoy the positive things in your life when you live consciously in the present. A better feeling of serenity and satisfaction may arise from this.

23. Thank the business owners and bus drivers in your neighborhood who assist you.

It's simple to take for granted the folks that assist us on a daily basis. We encourage a more pleasant encounter by showing our thanks for their assistance, and this may make their day better and make the community as a whole happier.

24. Thank your family and friends for their kind gestures and little favors.

We often overlook the little things that our loved ones continuously do for us. Thanking your family and friends for their love, support, and care may greatly improve your relationships.

25. Post grateful words and pictures throughout your house to serve as a gratitude reminder.

Keep reminders of your gratitude all around you. Create a gratitude-inspiring vision board or print some motivational phrases and put them in areas that you will regularly visit.

26. Pay a visit to an older neighbor and tell them how grateful you are to have them in your life.

Our communities' senior citizens are a gold mine of knowledge and life experience.

Thank your senior neighbors for being a part of your life by calling or visiting them, and how much they appreciate the gesture may surprise you.

27. Give your grandparents a call and tell them how much you care.

Grandparents are often disregarded, yet they may provide a lot of knowledge and direction. Call them to thank them for all they've done for you and to convey your love.

28. Accept obstacles and use them as chances for development.

When presented with difficulty, please make an effort to see it as a chance for development.

Keep a positive outlook and focus on the learning opportunities presented by the experience. You may improve your resilience and uncover new answers with the aid of this mentality change.

29. When you discover something new, be grateful.

Every new skill you acquire provides a chance to express gratitude, and learning is a lifetime process. Be grateful for the instructors and mentors who helped you along the journey and the value of your education.

30. Consider your mistake as a chance to learn.

We all make mistakes but try to look at them as teaching moments rather than focusing on them. Think about the lessons you can take away from the mistakes and how you can use those lessons to improve yourself.

31. Encourage your friends to see the good in everything.

Be there for your pals if they tend to focus on the bad things in life and attempt to encourage them to see the positive aspects of life. Invite them to express gratitude alongside you.

32. Keep in mind your friends who are there for you when things become tough.

Focus on the individuals that are there to support you rather than what is wrong. Please spend some time expressing your gratitude for their support and affection.

33. When life is treating you nicely, assist others.

Make time to assist others when things in your life are going well. Volunteer to assist individuals in need or carry out random acts of kindness. Your kindness may have a profound impact on someone else's life.

34. By cutting out images of all you have to be thankful for, make a gratitude collage

Create a collage using images of the things you are thankful for and organize them in a pleasing pattern. As an example of all the positive things in your life, put it on display in your room.

35. To develop the practice of gratitude, do it at exactly the same time each day.

Practice being grateful regularly and at the exact same time each day to help it become a habit. Do this in the morning or before bed. Making gratitude a daily habit makes it simpler to recall and ultimately develops into habitual behavior.

36. Think about your advantages.

By concentrating on your assets and the good things in your life, you may develop a spirit of gratitude, and this will improve your self-esteem and assist you in appreciating and being thankful for what you have.

37. Tell your loved ones and friends about the advantages of gratitude.

Sharing the advantages of gratitude with loved ones and friends may motivate and prod others to act in the same way. Discuss how being grateful has improved your life and how others might practice gratitude in their own lives.

By adopting these routines into our everyday lives, we may build a mindset of plenty and thankfulness even during challenging circumstances. Each act of gratitude, regardless of whether it be expressing appreciation to those who help us or observing the wonders of nature, can have a profound effect on our sense of well-being and interpersonal connections.

So, adopt these straightforward yet effective gratitude practices to lead a happier and more fruitful life.

EXPRESSION OF GRATITUDE

I wanted to take a moment to express my sincere gratitude to you for purchasing and reading my book. I hope that this book provided you with some value and that you enjoyed reading it.

I would be truly grateful if you could take a few minutes to leave a positive review on Amazon.

By sharing your experience, you can provide valuable insights and information that can assist others in making an informed decision.
Your review doesn't have to be long, just a sentence or two about what you liked about the book would be incredibly helpful.

Your feedback and support are incredibly valuable to me, and I appreciate it more than words can express, and I hope to continue creating work that you find valuable, informative, educative, and enjoyable.

Scan the ***QR code*** below to leave a review

CONCLUSION

Thank you for reading this book.

The life skills and the teen boy's capacity-building activities I discussed in this book are the essential learning instrument for survival, capacity growth, and a wonderful life for teen boys.

Cultivating and implementing these life skills promotes healthy social, emotional, and cognitive development, the capacity to develop the right positive attitude, make the right decision, develop strong work ethics, develop good communication skills, practice empathy and gratitude, set realistic and achievable goals, manage stress and anxiety, take responsibility for their actions, and deal with the constantly increasing speed and change of contemporary life.

To transition into strong and independent adults, you need to make the life skills you have learned in this book your guiding principle and apply them daily.

BOOKS BY V GODFREY

VISIT **VGODFREY.COM** OR SCAN THE ***QR CODE*** BELOW

You can connect with V Godfrey at:

Email: victor.godfrey.u@gmail.com

Facebook DM Link: https://m.me/V.U.GODFREY

Instagram: @v.u.godfrey

REFERENCES

https://www.skillsyouneed.com/ips/improving-communication.html

https://professional.dce.harvard.edu/blog/eight-things-you-can-do-to-improve-your-communication-skills/

https://www.oberlo.com/blog/communication-skills

https://www.stevenson.edu/online/about-us/news/importance-effective-communication/

https://sanjeevdatta.com/hygiene-tips-for-teenage-boys/

https://healthguide.ng/hygiene-tips-for-teenage-guys/

https://modernteen.co/guide-to-personal-hygiene-for-teens/

https://www.indeed.com/career-advice/career-development/conflict-resolution-strategies

https://www.clackamas.us/ccrs/resolve.html

https://www.linkedin.com/pulse/how-resolve-conflict-10-steps-g-and-h-management-services

https://www.uopeople.edu/blog/how-to-improve-teamwork-skills/

https://www.careeraddict.com/improve-teamwork-skills-workplace

https://www.canr.msu.edu/news/increase_youth_employability_through_teamwork_skills

https://www.momjunction.com/articles/team-building-activities-games-and-exercises-for-teens_00375666/

https://www.noomii.com/articles/809-8-simple-steps-to-good-decisionmaking-for-teens

https://wellspringprevention.org/blog/help-child-develop-decision-making-skills/

https://www.indeed.com/career-advice/career-development/how-to-improve-decision-making

https://www.apa.org/topics/resilience/bounce-teens

https://www.verywellmind.com/ways-to-become-more-resilient-2795063

https://parentandteen.com/building-resilience-in-teens/

https://www.health.harvard.edu/mind-and-mood/six-relaxation-techniques-to-reduce-stress

https://paradigmtreatment.com/relaxation-techniques-teen/

https://www.newportacademy.com/resources/well-being/relaxation-skills-for-teens/

https://www.forbes.com/sites/bernardmarr/2022/08/05/13-easy-steps-to-improve-your-critical-thinking-skills/

https://www.risepreneur.com/developing-critical-thinking-skills-of-a-teenager/

https://www.masterclass.com/articles/taking-responsibility-for-your-actions

https://www.trackinghappiness.com/how-to-take-responsibility-for-your-actions/

https://themindfool.com/take-responsibility-for-your-actions/

https://www.clarke.edu/campus-life/health-wellness/counseling/articles-advice/developing-a-positive-attitude/

https://getoffyourattitude.com/how-to-keep-a-positive-attitude-as-a-teenager/

https://www.risepreneur.com/having-a-positive-mental-attitude-as-a-teenager/

https://andrewsobel.com/article/eight-ways-to-improve-your-empathy/

https://www.verywellmind.com/how-to-develop-empathy-in-relationships-1717547

https://www.indeed.com/career-advice/career-development/how-to-improve-listening-skills

https://www.forbes.com/sites/womensmedia/2012/11/09/10-steps-to-effective-listening/?sh=1f8f22953891

https://www.futurelearn.com/info/blog/general/7-ways-improve-your-listening-skills

https://evolve-mma.com/blog/4-reasons-why-learning-self-defense-is-important-for-children/

https://m.timesofindia.com/life-style/parenting/moments/top-self-defence-techniques-you-need-to-teach-your-child/photostory/84403284.cms

https://www.parentcircle.com/self-defense-techniques-for-kids/article

https://www.ccl.org/articles/leading-effectively-articles/achievable-personal-goals-align-with-values/

https://timeular.com/blog/why-is-important-set-realistic-goals/

https://www.indeed.com/career-advice/career-development/how-to-set-realistic-goals

https://coggno.com/blog/ways-to-improve-your-work-ethic/

https://www.linkedin.com/pulse/7-ways-develop-strong-work-ethic-get-ahead-by-linkedin-news

https://www.creativesystems.com/the-importance-of-physical-activities-for-teens/

https://www.wikihow.com/Be-Physically-Fit

https://www.newportacademy.com/resources/empowering-teens/power-of-gratitude/

https://www.conehealth.com/services/behavioral-health/outpatient-behavioral-health-care/7-benefits-of-gratitude/

Printed in Great Britain
by Amazon